To: Henry A. Rosenberg, Jr

A Great Baltimorean

Harold G. Rukert
11/15/82

THE PORT
Pride of Baltimore

Overleaf Illustration: Fort McHenry, 1820 Robert G. Merrick Print Collection, Maryland Historical Society

THE PORT
Pride of Baltimore

NORMAN G. RUKERT

Published by Bodine & Associates, Inc.
Baltimore, Maryland • 1982

Also by Norman G. Rukert
The Fells Point Story (1976)
Historic Canton (1978)
Federal Hill (1980)

First Edition
Library of Congress Catalog No. 82-7067A
SBN 910254-17-6
Copyright 1982 by Bodine & Associates, Inc.
Printed in the U.S.A.

INTRODUCTION

THE WORLD, or at least the North American Continental portion of it, now recognizes the City of Baltimore as a symbol of urban rebirth.

What has been accomplished on the shores of the Patapsco River in the past several decades equates in a modest degree to the mandate of Aristotle in his *Politics*.

"... The end of the State is the good life and these are the means towards it. ... The State is a union of families and villages in a perfect and self-sufficing life."

Now, while Baltimore has not quite reached the pinnacle Aristotle established or reached the sublime goals of St. Augustine's *City of God*, it has restored the nation's faith in the viability of the City as a good place to live one's life.

This happy condition is due to many factors but the first of these is that Baltimore is a *port* city. It owes its birth, its adolescence and its historical maturity to this singular fact.

Through wars, political and economic metamorphosis, the City has been intrinsically fused with its port.

Few who live in this port city appreciate the fact they are breathing, playing, working in an international center of commerce, much less that they find themselves living out their time on this planet here in Baltimore because nature and men made it a world port.

One of the rare few is the author of this book. He and thousands of others each day of their lives work in and for this city on its docks and on the some 6,000 ships that seek out Baltimore from every trade route of the world.

With this book, he does what should have been done before—he documents and salutes our heritage—the port.

No one has more valid credentials for this task. The author is an offspring of a true Baltimore port family. The Rukerts are an outstanding example of citizens who pledged their troth in the enduring marriage of city and port.

W. Gregory Halpin, Maryland Port Administrator

CONTENTS

ACKNOWLEDGMENTS

As with my three previous histories, preparation and publication of this volume was made possible by the enthusiasm, interest, and cooperation of a number of individuals.

Katharine Chatard, Carol Ernst and Anne Macsherry assisted in the research spending many hours at the Maryland Department of the Enoch Pratt Free Library and the Maryland Historical Society.

The staffs of many institutions were most helpful; I mention especially Dr. Morgan Pritchett and the Maryland Department of the Pratt Library and Lewis A. Beck and Nancy Brennan of the Radcliffe Maritime Museum at the Maryland Historical Society and Laura Brown at the Langsdale Library of the University of Baltimore.

Frank Pilachowski and Harry Connolly, two excellent photographers, did a fine job reproducing useful photographs from old negatives.

The following articles from the *Maryland Historical Magazine* were used: "The Observatory of Federal Hill," by M. V. Brewington, March, 1949; "The Amazing Colonel Zarvona," by Charles A. Earp, March, 1939.

From time to time, informative articles have appeared in various magazines and newspapers. *Baltimore Magazine* published the following: "Queer Ships that Sailed the Bay," by William C. Steuart, February, 1964 and "The Story of the Fertilizer Industry in Baltimore," April, 1938.

Thanks are due James V. Guthrie, who spent his entire career on the waterfront and has written three fine manuscripts: "History of the Steamship Trade of Baltimore," "History of the Propeller Club of Baltimore," and "Automation on the Waterfront."

My thanks to George S. Goodhues, Jr. for the details supplied on the "Alum Chime" disaster of 1913. I also made use of the Baltimore *Sun* files of March 8, 1913.

I am indebted to the Maryland Port Administration and the Greater Baltimore Committee, Inc. W. Gregory Halpin, Maryland Port Administrator, and Donald Klein, Director of Port Promotion and Public Information Officer, were most gracious in providing important data and pictures. David Gillece and the staff at the Greater Baltimore Committee supplied reports and statistics that were most helpful.

Many other individuals helped in the gathering of important information . . . Lois Bourquin, Public Affairs Office, U.S. Customs Service . . . Both the Philadelphia and Baltimore offices of the U.S. Corps of Engineers for pictures and data on dredging Baltimore harbor . . . Captain Thomas J. Murphy, Jr. who supplied information on the early captains of the coffee fleet . . . and a classmate, Robert H. Burgess who spent many years at the Mariners Museum, (Newport News, Virginia) and is author of numerous fine books on the Chesapeake Bay.

To Harold A. Williams, retired assistant managing editor of the *Baltimore Sun*, and author of *The Western Maryland Railway Story* and *Baltimore Afire*, my sincere gratitude for his editing skill and his helpful suggestions in compiling this volume.

Norman G. Rukert

ILLUSTRATIONS

THE FIRST CENTURY: 1750–1850

THE ARK AND THE DOVE sailed up the Chesapeake Bay in 1634 carrying the first Maryland settlers for Lord Baltimore's province. For many years the colonists' chief occupation was farming, mainly the growing of tobacco. About the only towns were St. Marys, the first settlement, and Providence, later known as Annapolis. After the Maryland Assembly in 1683 urged that more towns be established, a number were started, but only one, Joppa, on the Little Gunpowder, lasted long, and that for only 50 years. In 1706 the Assembly made Whetstone Point (now Fort McHenry) a port of entry, the first within the present limits of Baltimore. In the early 1700's several Baltimore countians petitioned the Assembly for a town on the Patapsco at Moale's Point, owned by John Moale. He did not want a town on his land, which he felt was rich in iron ore, and, as a member of the Assembly, he was able to defeat such a bill. The would-be-incorporators then picked Cole's Harbor on the Northwest Branch of the Patapsco. A bill creating Baltimore Town was passed by the Assembly and signed by the governor, Benedict Leonard Calvert, on August 8, 1729. A town of 60 acres was laid out on land owned by two brothers, Charles and Daniel Carroll.

At this time the settled portion of British America consisted of a strip of seaboard more than 1,200 miles in length but not many miles inland. The combined population of the twelve colonies was about 250,000 including slaves but not counting Indians. Philadelphia, although but recently founded, had a population of more than 10,000 and was the largest city in America. New York had a population of about 5,000, Boston about 7,000.

The new Baltimore Town grew slowly, and so did its port.

Col. J. Thomas Scharf noted in "Chronicles of Baltimore" for the year 1723— "In this year there were but five ships in the Patapsco up for freight for London, to which place the trade was then carried on extensively, but one of which ships was said to lie in the Northern Branch. There were persons living in the last 20 years who have seen as many vessels of burthen anchored at the same time, at the point between the south and middle branches of the Patapsco, as in the north branch on which our city was finally established. The ships which traded with the surrounding country never at this time ascended the Patapsco, but lying at anchor off North Point, received their cargoes from the rivers which emptied into the Bay in the vicinity."

And for the year 1739, Scharf wrote, "On the 29th of August Captain Michael Willson, of the good ship *Parad and Gally*, published according to law that he was up for freight; and it appears from the records that he received one hogshead of leaf tobacco, shipped by Avarila Day, and consigned to Messrs. Delmitt and Heathwat of London, at the rate of seven pounds sterling per ton. This is the first vessel we find in the records of Baltimore County published according to law for freight."

Baltimore in 1752 by John Moale

As late as 1748 only seven ships came into the Northwest Branch and advertised for cargo in the *Maryland Gazette* of Annapolis, as required by law.

A turning point came about two years later. This is how it happened.

In 1745 a ship docked in Philadelphia; among the passengers were two young Irishmen named Stevenson. Both were physicians, educated at Oxford and therefore presumably not impecunious. The ship they had sailed on came to load not tobacco, but flour. That is why it sailed up the Delaware. Little tobacco was grown in Pennsylvania, for tobacco was a difficult crop both to grow and to transport. Because of tobacco's dependence on slave and indentured labor it implied a form of social and economic organization as distasteful to the Quakers scattered along the Delaware as to the Germans who were settling farmlands near Philadelphia. That land was especially suited to the growing of wheat, and its streams provided sites for mills. When the Stevensons arrived a wheat boom was taking place in Pennsylvania. But little was shipped to England because of the Corn Laws, which put a heavy impost on imported wheat except in times of great scarcity, limiting that market. Yet Ireland, especially Northern Ireland, was a growing one.

The two young doctors were born in Londonderry; John in 1718 and his brother Thomas two or three years later. They were Presbyterians, not Quakers, and maybe that is why, instead of taking up grants in Pennsylvania, they settled in Maryland. Dr. Thomas purchased property just outside the limits of Baltimore Town and built a fine house. It was by far the most imposing structure in the community. He called it "Parnassus," but the cynical townsfolk, discouraged because their town had not yet justified itself, nicknamed it "Stevenson's Folly."

Part of his medical knowledge was applicable to an immediate problem—smallpox. He knew that a man inoculated with the mild disease called cowpox was thereafter immune to the more dangerous ailment it resembled. A year after he moved into his new house, a smallpox epidemic struck the community. He persuaded a few townspeople to try his new method, using Parnassus as a hospital during the period of their infection. The results were so encouraging that his place in the community was established.

History does not record whether his brother John was a good physician or not. In any event we know he was a great wanderer and soon, despite the bad quality of the few roads, got to know the country round about much better than most of the older inhabitants. He did not fail to notice the manifold problems harrassing tobacco growers. He lived through at least one period when tobacco prices in London hardly paid the freight. He remembered the thriving business in wheat and flour which was being carried on between Philadelphia and his native Ireland.

As the Stevenson home was on the muddy road winding down from York, he had the opportunity to talk with dejected Germans who had been persuaded to settle along that road in the belief that they would make fortunes from tobacco. He also travelled as far west as Frederick, where tobacco planters were struggling with the almost impossible task of getting their product to tidewater. As he walked along the many swift-flowing streams which ran down the hills into the muddy and inconsequential harbor of Baltimore Town he noted, as an alert man would, that the small mills grinding their own flour could just as easily work twenty-four hours a day every day of the week and every week of the year instead of the occasional few hours they were used.

Dr. John Stevenson, in brief, saw the obvious—what their own addiction to tobacco and the manorial culture founded on tobacco had blinded the planters of the upper shores of the Chesapeake Bay to.

John Stevenson   *From the television show "The Port that Built a City"*

He wrote a letter to a friend in Ireland about the possibility of shipping a cargo of flour. The reply was favorable; a ship was being dispatched to load flour. This news was perhaps the most significant information received in Baltimore before or since, as far as its port was concerned. He immediately set about contracting for vast quantities of flour. The word "vast" is used relatively, for up to that time the planters had grown wheat grudgingly and almost entirely for their own use. Unaccustomed to dealing in such a commodity, they may have accepted Stevenson's predictions with misgivings; still, they had little to lose and everything to gain.

Almost certainly it was in 1750 that the ship finally arrived and discharged her cargo. It probably used bricks for ballast, for the credit of Maryland planters was not good then. The vessel docked at Fells Point because the harbor of Baltimore Town was not deep enough for most ocean-going vessels. Two weeks later the vessel sailed for Ireland with a full cargo of flour.

Now that the vessel had cleared and was on her way, there was nothing for Dr. John Stevenson to do but wait. It is probable that, with his sanguine temperament, he began to figure repaying the planters who had entrusted their flour to him and estimating his own possible profits. He may have made tentative contracts for further cargoes should the venture be successful.

And it was successful! Word came from his correspondent that the flour had been sold at a good price and that further cargoes could likewise be disposed of. Dr. Stevenson gave up his practice and became a merchant. He built a house in Baltimore Town on the south side of Long Street at Grant Alley. Behind the house, toward the marshes, he built a warehouse. Then he redoubled his efforts to promote the growth and shipment of flour through the port.

This marked the real beginning of the Baltimore port. It is true that if Dr. John Stevenson had not thought of the idea someone else would almost certainly have stumbled upon it. But it was he who conceived it and got the trade underway. From then on Baltimoreans knew this town had a future. Moreover, they knew what was to be its economic foundation. Baltimore was to be the port for the exportation of flour.

In 1771, Robert Eden arrived in Maryland as the new governor. One of his first distinguished guests was General Sir William Draper, who was making a tour of the colonies. General Draper had heard of Baltimore and asked to be taken to see it. Governor Eden quickly obliged as he himself would be visiting Baltimore for the first time. They demanded to know who was responsible for the growing town, its bustling port, its general air of knowing where it was going and why. The townspeople brought forward Dr. John Stevenson, whereupon Sir William Draper, in a graceful and elegant speech, bestowed upon him the title of "the American Romulus."

Demand for Maryland grain immediately boomed. Planters rapidly shifted to wheat, and the trade of the port changed. Flour milling became one of the paramount industries. It is interesting to note that by examining the port records at Annapolis from 1757 to 1773, the rising importance of Baltimore's port is reflected in the constantly increasing shipments of grain, while those of tobacco remain relatively static.

Other factors stimulated the rapid growth of the port. In the late 1760's the Fells Point area of Baltimore began to build ships and within 20 years would become the center of shipbuilding in Maryland.

William Fell, a Quaker by birth and a carpenter by trade, left Lancashire, England in 1730 to sail for Baltimore. That same year he purchased from Lloyd Harris a 100-acre tract called Copus Harbor, known at least as far back as 1670 as Long Island Point. Here in the vicinity of Lancaster Street he erected a mansion and a small shipyard to build two-masted sloops—a humble forerunner of the shipbuilding center Baltimore would become.

As soon as the lots on the Point were designated, Mark Alexander, Benjamin Nelson, George Wells and James Morgan each bought one and established a shipyard. The ideal location of the Point, and the proximity of large timber tracts with white oak, locust and red cedar, contributed to the growing shipbuilding industry. Georgia pine, naval stores, and iron manufactured at nearby foundries, were easily accessible. The labor force swelled when an influx of Acadians settled at Fells Point, many becoming ship carpenters and mariners.

These early shipbuilders designed the most romantic and historical vessel in United States history, the Baltimore Clipper. Using the Jamaican sloop as a model, Baltimore builders made technical refinements, the most notable of which was the change from sloop to schooner rig. The chief characteristics of the craft were long, light and extremely raking masts, little rigging, low freeboard, great rake to stem and stern posts, with a great deal of drag to the keel aft. The deadrise was great and bilges slack, beams usually great for their length, nearly always flush-decked. The craft had wide, clear decks suitable for working the ship and handling the guns.

At the outbreak of the Revolution, Baltimore was young, aggressive, and ready for anything. As rival merchants to the north became weakened by the non-importation agreements directed at British policies, those in Baltimore, for the most part, held their own. While His Majesty's Royal Navy blockaded other major Eastern seaports, the Virginia Capes were left unguarded. This was due to a shortage of warships, since most British naval forces were tied up in England's European wars, although a single frigate could have done the job. It is possible to suspect that the Admiralty lords with the tacit support of the English ruling class, who loved their after-dinner pipes of fine

Baltimore Clipper

Maryland Historical Society

Maryland and Virginia tobacco, did not press the commander of their Atlantic fleet too hard to seal off their supplies. It was, after all, a gentlemen's war. In any event, astute Baltimoreans took advantage of their freedom to develop still more new markets in the West Indies and Latin America. As a result, their industry and commerce profited enormously and Baltimore was on the way to maritime importance.

During the war, Maryland, and Baltimore in particular, took the lead in privateering. From April 1, 1777 to March 14, 1783, 248 privateers, furnished with letters of marque and reprisal, sailed out of the Bay carrying a total armament of 1,810 guns—a formidable fleet for even the greatest navy in the world to run down. The profits derived from their prizes was a lucrative source of wealth for their owners. In addition, capital tended to concentrate in Baltimore from other blockaded ports.

A privateer was a privately-owned vessel, armed and manned at her owner's expense for the purpose of capturing enemy merchant craft in time of war. International law required that she have a commission, or letter-of-marque, from her government, otherwise she would be considered a pirate. To obtain a letter-of-marque a vessel had to be bonded to the government to satisfy any claims that might arise from illegal captures; two bondsmen were needed for each privateer. Theoretically, the privateer had no right to her prizes until they were condemned by due process of law, but as the privateer could destroy vessels at sea, this was a mere formality. The owner, officers and crew held shares in the privateering enterprises. Privateers usually carried two classes of men—the "gentlemen seamen," who came from good families, enjoyed privileges on board and "typical privateers," who were free-lance men-of-war. The obvious differences between the two groups generated many clashes and mutinies aboard privateers were frequent.

After a peace treaty was signed, many of the privateers were sold to French or Spanish interests in the Caribbean, but many continued to raid British commerce under the command of adventurers. Commerce was sluggish for the next few years, limited principally to trade with the West Indies in smaller vessels, while large ones were being constructed for foreign trade. Industrious merchants continued to move to Baltimore from the north thus contributing to the rapidly growing spirit of enterprise which, more than anything else, caused shipping to concentrate at Baltimore instead of at the more logical but less energetic port of Norfolk. The failure of European grain crops added a further stimulus to trade. Perhaps even more important was the confidence instilled by the adoption of the Constitution. Capital increased, shipbuilding and all branches of industry expanded. Baltimore was rapidly challenging the older ports of Philadelphia, New York and Boston and was attracting widespread notice.

T. Courtenay J. Whedbee in his book, "The Port of Baltimore in the Making, 1828–1878," declared, "Brissot de Warville, writing of his travels in the United States in 1788, commented that 'a great deal of trade of Philadelphia has passed there.' This learned Frenchman already realized the importance of the Susquehanna Valley to Baltimore and continued:

'Many foodstuffs go down there by the Susquehanna. When that river is navigable, Baltimore will be an important place.'

By 1790, seven regularly scheduled packet services were sailing from Baltimore to other East Coast ports. Shipments "of wheat had now risen to an annual export of 228,062 bushels in addition to 127,284 barrels of flour and 5,588 barrels of bread. Moreover, a large export trade was also being carried on in corn, beans, peas, lumber, corn meal, tobacco, and flaxseed. Such rapid growth, which would soon appear small in comparison with the next four decades, inspired a would-be poet 400 miles northward to write:"

> *Torn from herself,*
> *where depth her soil divide,*
> *and Chesapeake intrudes her angry tide,*
> *Gay Maryland attracts the wandering eye,*
> *A fertile region with a temperate sky,*
> *In year elapsed, her heroes of renown*
> *From British Anna named her favorite town*
> *But lost her commerce, tho' she guards their laws,*
> *Proud Baltimore that envi'd commerce draws*
> *Few are the years since then, at random placed*
> *Some wretched huts her happy port disgraced*
> *Safe from all winds, and covered from the bay*
> *There at his ease the lazy native lay*
> *How rich and great, no more a slave to sloth*
> *She claims importance from her hasty growth,*
> *High in renown, her streets and homes arranged*
> *A group of cabins to a city changed*
> *Tho' rich at home, to foreign lands they stray*
> *For foreign trappings trade their wealth away.*

In 1794 Congress passed a bill which President Washington signed on March 27 authorizing the construction of six frigates. The naval captain named by Henry Knox, secretary of war, as captain of one ship was Thomas Truxton, a former successful privateersman during the Revolution. One of his responsibilities was to choose a site on which to build the ship, one of the largest ever to be constructed in this country. He finally selected Stodder's yard on Harris Creek in the port of Baltimore.

The first step was to prepare the yard by laying down gravel and pilings as a base for the vessel. Shortly after this was done, the plans arrived and laborers were employed. But building the ship was no easy feat. Months would pass before the shipwrights could locate enough live timber, curved to fit the specifications. Once the timber was procured, however, Truxton and Stodder battled over the design of the vessel. Other arguments also delayed the work so much that she was the farthest behind all of the frigates being built.

But finally, on September 7, 1797, the ship was launched and christened the *Constellation*. She sailed from Baltimore on June 26, 1798, the first to put to sea under the bill Congress had passed four years earlier. (Ever since it has provided a debate among naval historians as to whether the frigate, now restored and moored permanently in Baltimore's Inner Harbor, is or isn't the oldest U.S. warship afloat).

In 1797 Captain David Porter, who had served in privateers during the Revolution, announced he would construct a marine observatory on Federal Hill. Porter planned to provide a system to announce the impending arrival of vessels while they were still miles downriver. His scheme was simple and quickly gained acceptance. Ships entering the Patapsco would hoist their house flag which could easily be seen from the observatory with the aid of a powerful telescope. A duplicate house flag was then run aloft on the observatory's flagpole, signalling the maritime community of its arrival. When a second vessel hove in sight, a small cannon was fired to alert the port to a change in or addition to the flag hoist.

Captain David Porter's Observatory, Federal Hill

Baltimore Sunpapers

On June 7, 1899, the current proprietor, Marcus Dudley, sold his interest to the Chamber of Commerce which set up a telephone system linking its offices with Cove Point, far down the Bay, to get the entries through the Capes, and another line to North Point to gain news of the upper Bay traders. One hundred two years of faithful service had been rendered by the flags and telescopes. Now their day had passed. As if the very building knew the work was finished, on July 20, 1902, amid a crash of thunder as loud as the guns that had heralded its opening, and with flashes of lightning reminiscent of "bombs bursting in air," the lookout house toppled and fell apart during a summer squall.

The French Revolution, the general European wars, and the revolt in Santo Domingo which soon followed, had tremendous repercussions upon the commerce of Baltimore. The hundreds of refugees who flocked to the city from that Caribbean capital added a stimulating element to the life of the city, and strengthened its business and personal ties with the West Indies. As America began to take over the European carrying trade, Baltimore received more than her share because of the swiftness of her vessels. Used as a transshipment point for West Indies sugar and molasses to avoid the British blockade, nearly two-thirds of her exports and imports were of foreign origin.

The Baltimore port experienced a phenomenal increase in shipping during the 1790's. In 1791, 325 vessels arrived from foreign ports and 5,464 bay craft docked here. In 1797 shipping amounted to 59,837 tons, and by 1798 export cargoes alone amounted to over $121,000,000. The Baltimore shipyards, merchants and shipowners had reason to be optimistic for the future at the close of the century.

Some historians consider the first half of the nineteenth century as the golden age of Baltimore. The city grew and prospered—Baltimore in 1800 had reached a population of 31,514, a 125 per cent increase in ten years.

By 1801 the European and West Indies demand for wheat and flour had become so great that incorporated road-building companies constructed the Frederick, York, Falls Road and Reisterstown turnpikes to facilitate the hauling of grain and flour to the port. Thus the hinterland sent over these turnpikes an endless supply of its bounty which formed the cargoes for the speedy Baltimore Clippers. It is to the turnpike and the clipper, then, that the Baltimore port largely owes its rapid growth during these years.

The Maryland Legislature authorized the building of a hospital on Lazaretto Point in Lower Canton in 1801 for the treatment of smallpox, then a major health problem. The first quarantine station for the port also was built and remained there until 1870 when the U. S. Government moved the station to Hawkins Point.

Commerce brought continued prosperity until the Peace of Amiens in 1801 which meant that merchant vessels of both England and France were free once more to carry the products of their respective nations without danger of molestation. The Embargo of 1807 had a depressing effect, but on the whole Baltimore suffered less than rival ports because her vessels were still able to elude British blockades and consequently received enormous profits and special licenses from the French Government.

No longer an obscure small town, Baltimore gained an international reputation as a financial center with the expansion of the import firms of Robert Oliver and Alexander Brown in investment and foreign banking. By 1812, *Niles Weekly Register*, published in Baltimore, one of the most influential journals of its day, reported that, within a mere three decades, Baltimore had risen "from absolute insignificance to a degree of commercial importance which has brought down upon it the envy and the jealousy of all the great cites of the Union."

When war was declared against England on June 18, 1812, Baltimore not only contributed to the Federal Navy, but it also resumed its profitable business of privateering. Within four months 42 privateers had sailed from Baltimore, carrying 330 guns and 3,000 men. Its shipyards had refined the Baltimore Clipper to near perfection, and as a privateer it was without equal. During the war 126 privateers operated out of Baltimore, capturing over 500 British ships. Among the most successful privateers were the *Rossie*, which in 45 days took prizes worth over $1,000,000; the *Rolla*, seizing prizes worth over $2,000,000; the *Comet* which captured 35 British ships and, the most famous of all, the *Chasseur*, the "Pride of Baltimore" which took prizes worth well over $3,000,000. The total value of all prizes was estimated at $16,000,000.

Members of Parliament, referring to the privateers, termed Baltimore "this nest of vipers." A British statesman called Baltimore "the great depository of the hostile spirit of the United States against England" and a British admiral predicted that it "was a doomed town." And it seemed like one.

The Federal government, lacking money and manpower for a strong national defense, could not help the city; besides it had sent many of the town's young men on the fruitless Canadian campaign in 1812. Fort McHenry, which had been in a state of neglect, was hurriedly armed with second-hand cannon taken from an abandoned French frigate. All able-bodied men still remaining were called up to help defend the city and its approaches. After the British had captured Washington and burned public buildings, they landed an army on North Point while its fleet sailed up the Patapsco. The army was repulsed after a skirmish and the fleet, from a safe distance, launched more than 1,500 bombs on Fort McHenry, which could not reply because its borrowed guns did not have enough range. During the attack Francis Scott Key was inspired by the flag still flying over the fort to pen the words to the "Star-Spangled Banner," which later became our national anthem.

In 1819 work in the shipyards came to a halt because of the depression following the war. Inflation, the yellow fever epidemic and an abundance of Baltimore Clippers took a toll. Some desperate shipyards, unable to resist the chance for a profit, converted the Baltimore Clippers into ships suitable for the slave trade. Everything was sacrificed for speed; the lines of the ships were sharpened, the spars lengthened and sails added. Though the Federal government tried to intervene, Baltimore shipyards continued such conversions for years. It was a sad ending for so noble a vessel which twice had played a major role in winning and preserving our independence. Howard Chapelle, a well-known maritime author, has written: "Sired by war, mothered by privateering and piracy, and nursed by cruelty, nevertheless, the Baltimore Clipper will always remain the type representative of the highest development of small sailing craft built by American builders." The Baltimore Clipper had established the reputation of Baltimore shipyards as being among the finest in America.

It is ironic that the Baltimore-built frigate *Constellation*, the pride of old Baltimore shipbuilders, should have been sent to the Caribbean to search for other vessels of her home port and later to the Congo coast, where she captured, on September 26, 1860, the brig *Cora*, carrying 705 slaves.

While Baltimore had always enjoyed trade with other Chesapeake Bay ports, the introduction of steam led to its significant expansion. Sail-power on the Bay's many tributaries was, at best, tricky and rarely dependable, but steam provided both the needed reliability and ability to maneuver.

The Reeder Works, c 1887

Maryland Historical Society

One who contributed to the development of steam was Charles Reeder. He was born in Bucks County, Pa. on April 18, 1787, and in his early teens was apprenticed to a millwright and carpenter. Serving out his apprenticeship, he became a master of the trade. Feeling himself competent to take a position outside his trade, he went to work for Daniel Large, an early builder of steam engines who had worked with James Watt in England. Soon Reeder became a proficient machinist. He studied the design and use of the steam engine, and in 1813 was sent to Baltimore to supervise the installation of a steam engine in the *Chesapeake*, the first steamboat in Baltimore. The *Chesapeake*, built by William Flanigan in his shipyard at the foot of Market Street, was designed to run between Baltimore and Frenchtown on the Elk River in the upper bay—part of the route to Philadelphia. She was 130 feet long, had a twenty-two-foot beam, five-foot hold, and travelled five miles per hour. There was no pilot house or upper deck. The pilot stood in the bow and relayed his steering orders aft by calling or stamping on the deck. During the first year, she earned her owners a dividend of 40 per cent.

Reeder worked as a machinist until 1815, when he established a small steam engine factory in the Federal Hill area. His impact in the development of that area will be examined in a future chapter.

Had a bold plan that was proposed in 1838 been realized, Baltimore would not have its beautiful Harborplace today. In November of that year, Dr. Thomas H. Buckler proposed a novel plan to fill up the basin by leveling Federal Hill. Dr. Buckler contended that adoption of his proposal was necessary to the health of the city, and that commercial and financial advantage would also accrue. The removal of Federal Hill would not only extend the view from the city, but would permit fresh air from the river. Transportation between virtually separated parts of the city would be greatly facilitated, and land would be created which would, when sold and improved, add at least $9,000,000 to the city's tax base. The measure would also eliminate the noxious and pestilential waters of the shallow, stagnant basin.

Buckler's plan was laid before the City Council, debated, and referred to a committee. A report by Benjamin H. Latrobe demonstrated its financial practicality by showing the cost for actual filling to be only $764,346, not including the cost for damage to existing property rights. After much discussion in the press and great opposition from shoreline property owners, the plan was dropped.

The era of steam expanded Baltimore's seaborne trade, foreign and domestic, so it gave the port a tremendous boost by a vast expansion of its hinterland. The American frontier had advanced to the Mississippi River and well beyond; Fort Duquesne had long since become Pittsburgh, and former frontier settlements had grown to metropolitan dimensions. For the merchants of the eastern seaboard, the question was how to tap this swiftly growing market and, importantly, how to get there first. For some, the answer lay in the canal, expensive to build and not much better in speed or economy than the horse-drawn wagon.

Baltimore's western trade, however, was seriously menaced by the introduction of steam on the Ohio and the Mississippi in 1811. Previously, Baltimore had been the chief source of supplies to the west and southwest for heavier merchandise. However, with the opening of navigation on the Mississippi, these westerners found that shipment by water was more continuous and less toilsome and expensive than by wagon over Braddock's Road and the new turnpikes. So New Orleans became the great mart of exchange and supply, and Baltimore's commerce suffered accordingly.

More important to Baltimore was the opening of the Erie Canal in 1825. The effects of this waterway were enormous. Baltimore was jarred out of its listlessness and forced to embark on programs of internal improvements which were to have profound effects on the nation's transportation systems. Its immediate effect on the New York port was to open an immense hinterland. And it gave westerners a means of disposing of their "cash crops," the proceeds of which were used to buy New York goods. Thus, though they might ship to other ports, they usually bought their imports and domestic goods from New York. The effects of this were far-reaching. New York began to pay for western flour before it was milled, thus drawing a steady stream of wealth and trade. In two years Baltimore was forced out of the lead in the flour trade.

Baltimore's prestige in the western trade was assured so long as land routes, roadways and turnpikes were supreme; now she too must meet the challenge of canals, lest, as one pointed out, she will have "the difficulty of diverting trade after connections are once formed."

But, in line with their city's already established reputation for innovation, Baltimoreans saw their answer in the new-fangled railroad, demonstrated as workable in Great Britain. For one thing, a railroad would be cheaper to build; for another the experts were confidently predicting that a steam locomotive might someday be able to hurtle a string of cars along at speeds up to 15 miles an hour. Facts show that the plan of building the road was first conceived and discussed on February 12, 1827, at a meeting of 25 leading citizens of Baltimore, called together by George Brown, son of Alexander Brown, and held at his residence in Baltimore. The avowed purpose was to consider the best means of restoring trade which had been diverted by the introduction of steam navigation and the opening of the Erie and other canals to the West. As a result of this meeting, stock subscription books were opened on March 20, and 41,781 shares of stock almost immediately subscribed. The amount of money raised in Baltimore alone was $4,178,000.

In the spring of 1828, William Patterson and Columbus O'Donnell went to New York City to interest Peter Cooper, capitalist, philanthropist and inventor, in forming a real estate company to include all the waterfront property from Fells Point to Colgate Creek—3,000 acres for $105,000.

It was the commercial and industrial prospects of the Baltimore and Ohio Railroad, then under construction, that persuaded Cooper to invest in the new company. Mr. Cooper was led to believe that he was to pay one third of the cost and the other two men the balance. He soon discovered he was the only one who had put up any money.

In December, 1828, William Patterson, Francis Price, Ely Moore, Gideon Lee, Peter Cooper, James Ramsey and Columbus O'Donnell undertook to establish the Canton Company.

Columbus O'Donnell was the son of Captain John O'Donnell who originally settled the Canton area, which played an important role in the development of the port.

Captain John O'Donnell was born in 1749 in Limerick, Ireland. He had an adventurous life. At an early age he ran away to sea and, ending in India, amassed and lost a substantial fortune before he was 30. Within a few years he had accumulated another fortune, presumably by trading in the Orient.

The earliest evidence of his arrival in Baltimore is a notice in the *Maryland Journal and Baltimore Advertiser* on August 12, 1785:

"On Tuesday evening last there arrived here, directly from China, the Ship *Pallas*, commanded by its owner, Captain O'Donnell. She has on board a most valuable cargo, consisting of an extensive variety of teas, china, silks, satins, nankeens, etc. We are extremely happy to find the commercial reputation of this town so far increased, as to attract the attention of gentlemen who are engaged in carrying on this distant but beneficial trade."

The Maryland Journal also reported that O'Donnell was living in Fells Point during the time his cargo was offered for sale. There he probably met Sarah Chew-Elliott, the daughter of Captain Thomas Elliott. They were married on October 16, 1785. Baltimore treated the newcomer O'Donnell well: he sold his cargo at a good profit and found a wife.

Where the O'Donnells' first home was for the early months of their marriage is unknown. Sometime in 1786 O'Donnell bought eleven acres called Shoemakers Lot from Thomas Woodward. This was the beginning of a 1,981-acre estate around the elbow of the northwest branch of the Patapsco River, east from Fells Point to Lazaretto Point. The O'Donnell family house, which he called Canton, was probably built south of what is now Boston Street between Clinton Street and Highland Avenue, though some historians put it at Foster and Ellwood Avenues. The home was a long low one with a deep veranda, built in the style of an Indian official's home.

Actual work on the B & O Railroad was begun on July 4, 1828, and a great crowd gathered to witness the ground-breaking ceremonies. For the first few years the cars were to be pulled by horses until a dependable steam locomotive could be developed. On June 14, 1830 the railroad reached Ellicott's Mills, a distance of

Laying "first stone" of Baltimore & Ohio Railroad, 1828   *Enoch Pratt Free Library*

The Port—Pride of Baltimore / 25

thirteen miles. It should not be forgotten that these far-visioned men projected a railroad over the Allegheny Mountains to the Ohio River and inaugurated it with horse-drawn vehicles.

It was on August 30, 1830, that the first journey in America by steam was made over the road, from Baltimore to Ellicott's Mills. The locomotive, "Tom Thumb," which weighed only a ton and travelled 80 miles on a ton of coal, was built by Peter Cooper, who wrote this description of the historical event in a letter to William H. Brown:

"When I had completed the engine I invited the directors to witness an experiment. Some thirty-six persons entered one of the passenger cars and four rode on the locomotive, which carried its own fuel and water and made the first passage of thirteen miles, over an average ascending grade of eighteen feet to the mile, in one hour and twelve minutes. We made the return trip in fifty-seven minutes."

Despite many delays the railroad reached Frederick in 1832. As freight from Frederick steadily increased, three or four ships could often be seen in the port loading flour and other commodities from the interior.

In an effort to promote trade between Baltimore and the Susquehanna River region, the Baltimore and Susquehanna Railroad was incorporated on February 13, 1828, the purpose, as set forth in the charter, to build a railroad from Baltimore to York Haven, Pennsylvania (a point on the Susquehanna River about ten miles below Harrisburg). The railroad celebrated Baltimore City's centennial anniversary on August 8, 1829, by laying its cornerstone. This was some 60 feet from the present site of the North Avenue bridge. It was unearthed some 50 years later during excavations for the tunnel on the route to Washington. It marked the starting point of the second great highway of transportation to the port projected by the merchants of Baltimore.

The first six miles of the line was constructed along Jones Falls from Belvedere Street Depot (a few blocks east of the present Pennsylvania Station) to Relay Station (later Hollins) on Lake Roland. Regular service was inaugurated on July 4, 1831, with horses as motive power. This was scarcely more than a year after the Baltimore & Ohio Railroad had made history by opening its first thirteen miles from Mt. Clare to Ellicott's Mills.

Due to opposition from local interests, the Pennsylvania legislature at first refused to cooperate in the project. As a result, the Baltimore and Susquehanna management adopted an alternative plan of a route up the Green Spring Valley and on to Westminister, Maryland. The first seven miles from Relay (Hollins) to Green Spring Hotel (near Chattolanee) was opened on May 26, 1832; the line was quickly extended to Owings Mills. Meanwhile, the Pennsylvania legislature had modified its original attitude, and the Baltimore and Susquehanna again turned to its earlier goal. An extension from Relay Station to the York Turnpike at Timonium was opened September 13, 1832. Their first steam locomotive was built in England and placed in service on August 6, 1832. It was named the "Herald" after the ship which brought the tiny locomotive from Liverpool.

The Baltimore and Susquehanna Railroad reached York in 1838 which formed a short but vital link between the port and the rich farmlands of the Susquehanna Valley.

In the early 1800's Baltimore had an average of just 314 hours of fog on the Bay and only 194 hours at the mouth of the harbor—a great advantage when compared with New York's 876 hours. But the port had more ice than New York. The slow, brackish waters of the Patapsco River were more susceptible to freezing. For example, in 1831 nearly 100 vessels were ice-bound in the river and Bay. By 1835 the port had largely overcome this handicap by designing the country's first ice breaker, the *Relief*. It proved such a success that another was soon built by popular subscription.

In those days Baltimore was a ship-minded city. The lives and literature of the inhabitants were colored by the exploits of the vessels they sent to sea. During this period three Clipper ships, the *Ann McKim, Architect* and *Mary Whitridge*, attracted wide attention.

Clipper Ship Ann McKim

Maryland Historical Society

Of great significance in the history of Baltimore shipbuilding was the launching of the *Ann McKim* on June 4, 1833. Built by Kennard & Williamson at Philpot and Point Street for Isaac McKim, a Baltimore merchant, she rapidly became one of the most talked about of American sailing vessels. She was the forerunner of the illustrious fleet destined to make the American merchant marine known world-wide. McKim had her designed as a pet ship with little regard to cost. She was remarkably handsome, constructed of the finest materials with sparkling brass guns and fittings, and carrying three skysail yards and royal studding sails. Contrary to popular opinion, the *Ann McKim* was not the product of a single revolutionary genius, but the culmination of long development. Comparison of her draughts with those of earlier ships shows a striking similarity of ideas. She was merely more extreme, having greater drag to her keel and more exaggerated lines.

The *Ann McKim* sailed in the China trade for a number of years, and upon the death of Mr. McKim in 1837, was purchased by Howland & Aspinwall of New York. The vessel was not the first in the Clipper ship era and it did not directly influence shipbuilders, since no other ship was built like her. But it may have suggested the Clipper design in vessels of ship rig, and passing into the hand of Howland & Aspinwall, it undoubtedly hastened the opening of that era, as the first really extreme Clipper ship, the *Rainbow*, was owned by that firm.

The *Architect* was a Baltimore design of 520 tons built by Langley B. Culley at his Federal Hill shipyard and launched on August 28, 1848. She sailed light to New Orleans in January, 1849, and was soon filled with passengers and freight for San Francisco. Like many other vessels in the early months of 1849, most of the *Architect's* crew served without pay as a means of reaching the gold fields. The voyage proved eventful and tedious. Cholera broke out, causing several deaths among the 56 passengers. Dissensions arose, and the ship was obliged to put into Rio de Janeiro. Sailing again on March 18, she made slow time in the South Atlantic, encountered heavy weather off Cape Horn, and was reported to have put in a Chilean port for supplies and repairs, arriving at San Francisco on June 28, 1849. Some accounts state that this voyage consumed only 120 days actual sea time, a remarkable record for the time.

After making one more trip from New York to San Francisco, the *Architect* spent four years in trading between the West Coast of the United States and the Far East. Perhaps her most celebrated voyage occurred during the summer of 1853, when under the command of Captain George A. Potter, she sailed from Hong Kong with a

Architect

cargo of tea for London in the company of about a dozen English Clipper ships. After an astoundingly fast trip of only 107 days (against a monsoon), the *Architect* was able to sell her cargo before the appearance of the first of her rivals, whose captain, on entering the Thames, anxiously asked the pilot if he had seen anything of "a little American ship from Canton." By the time the *Architect* had returned to China, her reputation for speed was so great that she was chartered immediately to carry another cargo of tea to London at eight sterling per ton; this at a time when her English competition was glad to get three or four.

Mary Whitridge

Merchants Club of Baltimore

The *Mary Whitridge* was built in 1855 by Hunt & Wagner in Fells Point, for Thomas Whitridge, a Baltimore merchant. She was a 978-ton full-rigged ship, a new type which combined the stowage capacity of the old packet and the beauty and speed of the extreme Clipper ship. In the summer of 1855, under the command of Captain Cheeseborough, she left Baltimore for a voyage to England which would turn out to be one of the fastest passages in the history of sail. On board were a group of Baltimoreans, friends of Mr. Whitridge. On Sunday evening June 24, she left Cape Henry and reached the English Channel in twelve days and seven hours, having sailed 2,962 miles. This record has never been equalled by any sailing vessel.

On August 4, 1855 the *American and Commercial Advertisier* published this letter from a passenger:

"I doubt much whether any sailing vessel ever crossed the Atlantic in less time. This abundantly proves the admirable qualities of the noble ship and skill, seamanship, and fidelity of Captain Cheeseborough who tested thoroughly her merits. I am sure few parties have ever seen such favorable conditions—a swift, staunch ship, a skillful captain, delightful weather, a quick passage, a good tempered company—all combined to make the voyage long to be remembered."

Gold was discovered in California in 1848 and in Australia in 1851. When the East heard of these discoveries it seethed with excitement. Prospectors, adventurers and settlers clamored for passage. The demand for fast sturdy, cargo-carrying ships increased enormously. Freight rates leaped to unprecedented levels—the *Samuel Russel* in a single voyage earned over $70,000 in freight money alone. Steam powered vessels proved 48 days slower than the best Clipper journey from New York to San Francisco. Because of their international reputation and abundance of labor, the Baltimore shipbuilders were swamped with orders. In 1853 and 1854, eight Clippers were built in Baltimore, six of them, the *Flora Temple, Napier, Whistling Wind, Cherubin, Carrier Dover,* and the *Kate Hooper* ranging between 1,400 and 2,000 tons.

Even though some of the first ships to reach San Francisco during the gold rush were out of Baltimore, the port never really played an important role in that trade. Although during 1848 only two ships cleared the seaboard ports for San Francisco, one year later 775 joined the rush with only 38 out of Baltimore. By 1850 Baltimore had moved up to third place with 44 clearances, but still far behind New York and Boston.

One of the most celebrated of these California Clippers built in Baltimore by Edward & Richard Bell, was the diminutive *Seaman*, 500 tons. So successful was she that a sister ship, the *Seaman's Bride*, was launched the following year—of greater length, sharper lines and distinguished by the three moonsails above her skysails. She carried nearly 7,000 square yards of sail, an enormous area for her tonnage. These small Clippers were described in a local newspaper as "Winged witches of the waves."

It was with some justification that the New Orleans *Commercial Bulletin* said that the Baltimore shipyards turned out the "finest vessels in the world."

COFFEE, COPPER AND FERTILIZER: 1830-1892

COFFEE, COPPER ORE, and the raw materials to manufacture fertilizers, were three imports that contributed significantly to the growth of the port in the early nineteenth century.

It was through the pride of shipowners, masterful commanders and vigorous seamen, that a purely Baltimore enterprise was built in the '30's. This was the Brazilian Coffee Fleet.

The opening of the commercial markets with Brazil began before the Civil War but the trade did not reach its peak until after the seas were clear of Confederate privateers. Between 1835 and 1900, three ships, 48 barks, 11 barkentines, 11 brigs and two schooners were engaged in the coffee trade. Even with this number, many of which flew the house of a Baltimore merchant, other bottoms had to be chartered to meet the demand for outward and inward cargo. Coffee ships sailing out of Baltimore had many attractive names: *Adelaide, Virginia Dare, Priscilla, Carolina, Justina* and *Henrietta*. Masculine names were regarded as out of harmony with the world-wide gender of "she" as applied to ships. To men of the sea nothing is more beautiful or appropriate for a ship than a feminine name.

The coffee trade was the natural counterpart of the flour trade and constitutes a significant chapter in the history of the port. It was the most permanent, fundamental and successful element in Baltimore's import trade. Competition between the ports of Baltimore and New York was keen from 1835 to 1900. Since New York's western flour did not last long in tropical climates, ships leaving that port had difficulty in getting cargoes for the trip south. Baltimore offering flour from the mills of Hazall in Richmond, and products from Gambrill's in Ellicott's Mills and Ilchester assured the Clippers sailing out of the port a full cargo.

Most of the coffee fleet loaded and discharged their cargoes at Fells Point. The two largest warehouses and wharves were Brown's Wharf at the foot of Broadway and Belt's Wharf, foot of Fell Street. The first warehouse in the Brown's Wharf complex was built in 1816 by Joseph Biays, a Fells Point merchant. In 1840, George Brown, son of Alexander Brown, purchased this parcel plus surrounding properties from the Robert Oliver estate. He improved the warehouses and lengthened the pier— hence, the name Brown's Wharf. Belt's Wharf was built in 1845 by a group of local merchants and nearby canning companies combined. The most amazing thing is that both of these warehouses are still in use today. One can wander through the buildings, with beams and stanchions of Georgia pine, and still smell the aromatic odor of coffee impregnated in the timbers.

At Brown's Wharf, the Pendergast, Rollins, Whitridge, and Jenkins fleets discharged their cargoes from South America. Belt's Wharf was the terminal of the fleet of the Baltimore merchant C. Morton Stewart. Mr. Stewart had a partiality for

Josephine, of the Baltimore coffee fleet

Mariners Museum, Newport News, Va.

the barkentine-type vessel, while Mr. Rollins and the others held to the Baltimore-built bark model. The Baltimore vessels were built at Fells Point for this trade exclusively which gave them a reputation of being the cleanest and daintiest merchant craft afloat. Not all of these splendid ships were blessed with good luck.

The first *Josephine* was built at Belfast, Maine in 1892 for Mr. Stewart. On May 16, 1895, while bound from Rio de Janeiro with 9,000 bags of coffee consigned to Baltimore, she ran aground at night in thick weather at Little Island, south of Virginia Beach, Virginia. Life-saving crews from the nearby beach went to her aid and removed a number of her crew. A few men remained aboard as there was hope of refloating the vessel. A salvage company removed some of the cargo, but bad weather forced them to cancel operations. On the 18th, after being pounded by heavy seas, the *Josephine* finally capsized and was declared a total wreck.

Mr. Stewart had the second *Josephine* built in 1896 and it became the most successful vessel in the Baltimore Coffee Fleet. The sleek barkentine held the record by making the fastest passage from Rio de Janeiro to Baltimore. On November 26, 1897, she was reported off Cape Henry taking a pilot on board in 22 days from Sugar Loaf. The report was unbelievable to her owner and doubted by all the old sailors along the Fells Point waterfront. She continued in the coffee trade until after the turn of the century. Later she was sent to Philadelphia to be rigged as a four-masted schooner. On April 30, 1922, while bound from Jacksonville to Philadelphia with a cargo of lumber, she was found abandoned at sea by the Coast Guard cutter *Seminole*. She was towed to Southport, North Carolina and beached as a derelict.

Captain Benjamin F. Springsteen lived at 2038 Gough Street in Baltimore. He was master of the *Josephine* when she made her record-breaking trip from Brazil. The remarkably fast voyage attracted the attention of the shipping world, and the U. S. Navy obtained a chart of his voyage and a copy of the ship's log for reference.

On August 10, 1900, Captain Springsteen sailed from Baltimore as master of the barkentine *Priscilla* enroute to Brazil. On the seventeenth, a hurricane with winds of over 140 miles an hour, struck the *Priscilla* and carried her onto Gull Shoal.

The *Priscilla* broke into three pieces. All hands gathered on the quarter deck. Mrs. Springsteen, who was making her first trip to sea with the captain, was washed overboard and drowned. The captain's son, William Springsteen, mate of the vessel, was lost while trying to save his mother. Then the youngest child of the captain, Elmer Springsteen, was swept away by mountainous seas. Captain Springsteen, Second Mate Frank Mason and a crew member were saved, almost by a miracle, as the house of the vessel on which they were clinging was washed ashore.

On October 30, 1900 the captain's nineteen-year-old son, Howard Springsteen, was lost at sea during a trip from Port Spain, Trinidad to New York on the barkentine *Josephine*. He was standing on the ship's rail when a yard brace struck him and knocked him from the rail toward the sea. He managed to hold onto the brace and climbed back aboard the ship. That night the *Josephine* was struggling with a hurricane. The mate, Springsteen and several other sailors were on the main deck handling the sheet of the main staysail, which had gone adrift. The vessel was rolling heavily in high seas, while the wind blew about 70 miles an hour. The night was intensely dark. As the sail was flapping wildly in the hurricane the sheet rope wrapped itself about the chest of Springsteen, and, as the vessel rolled to the port, Springsteen was flung out to sea. When the vessel rolled back to starboard he was smashed against the side of the ship and knocked unconscious and disappeared in the darkness.

Captain Benjamin F. Springsteen died of a heart attack aboard the barkentine *Good News* and was buried at sea on January 21, 1901. The only survivor of the Springsteen family was a daughter, Mrs. Watson, who lived on South Chester Street.

The captains of the coffee fleet sailing out of Baltimore were a breed of their own. They were hard sailors of the old school, frequently performing miracles of dead reckoning, driving their vessels through fair weather and foul, but not too conservative to accept innovations. The perfect example was Captain Peter Erickson of the *Frances*. Ashore he was a sedate, well-dressed businessman, but once at sea he looked and acted like a pirate. In good weather he would read dime novels from his steamer chair near the wheel, clad in slippers, an old greasy cap and his pants rolled up to his knees. At three o'clock, up would come the cockney cook with the captain's "Tea," which consisted of a half pint of coffee and a huge doughnut. The captain would take his cup, spit out his chew of tobacco on the tray and tell the cook to "get the hell off the poopdeck." Sometimes he would make a little money on the side by smuggling diamonds and ostrich feathers out of Brazil - a frequent practice of these old skippers.

Another example was Captain William Forbes, commanding the *Albermarle* of the Whedbee Dickinson fleet. During one of his trips to Rio from Baltimore, he arrived during a revolution. The coffee fleet lay at anchor outside the harbor as the new government had closed the port. The harbor was protected by guns of the fort guarding the entrance. Captain Forbes decided that staying at anchor was a loss of time, so disregarding the fort's signals that he would be fired on if he tried to enter, he hoisted all sails and started into the port. The Brazilian officers were evidently too amazed to give the order to open fire as the *Albermarle* swept past in a cloud of canvas. The real reason, however, was that the new government did not wish to start any trouble with the United States. The *Albermarle* returned with the first cargo of the year and her exploit was discussed for many a day along the Fells Point waterfront. As late as 1922, a few of the old captains like Peter Eriksson and Edward Laplanche were still following their profession on the bridges of steamers.

After the turn of the century, Baltimore became second to New York as the chief port of coffee importation, as the latter offered a better distribution of the product. With the increased use of steam, the Baltimore coffee fleet was doomed. Only a few Clippers were sailing out of the Chesapeake Bay at the start of the Twentieth Century due to losses at sea, abandonment due to old age and conversion into barges. Among the latest Clippers to unload coffee in Fells Point were the *Grey Eagle, Gramaliel, Templar,* and *Yamayden.* So ended what has been termed the "Golden Era of the Coffee Fleet."

You need not be a Baltimorean to stand on the docks at Brown's Wharf or Belt's Wharf in Fells Point and dream of the days when one or two trim coffee Clippers were always taking on a cargo of flour or discharging bags of coffee from the plantations of Brazil. It is exciting to call up pictures of seas once dotted with Baltimore Clippers in gleaming canvas, tapering masts towering above graceful hulls, and remember that those captains and sailors worked these wharves. As Ruskin said, "A ship of sail is the only handiwork of man which harmonizes with Nature."

In 1804, Levi Hollingsworth, after studying (at times as a laborer) the English and Welsh copper industries, established the Gunpowder Copper Works on the Gunpowder Falls near what is now Harford Road and operated it until his death in 1822. Baltimore's shipbuilding industry was growing rapidly and required large quantities of copper spikes, bolts and rods, and later, copper sheathing to prevent barnacle growth.

Isaac McKim opened a steam-powered rolling mill on Smith's Wharf in 1827. Although his specialty was sheathing for ship bottoms, the steam engine, described as "stupendous," was also used to power the grindstones of a grist mill. In addition to this business, McKim helped the heirs of Hollingsworth operate the Gunpowder works. In 1845 the Baltimore and Cuba Smelting and Mining Company was incorporated by McKim's son, Haslett, with metallurgist Dr. David Keener as agent and technical adviser. This was the first time in this area a modern corporate structure and technical layout were used in the copper business. All operations from smelting to rolling were carried on, with steam power utilized throughout. The ore was imported from Chile and Cuba.

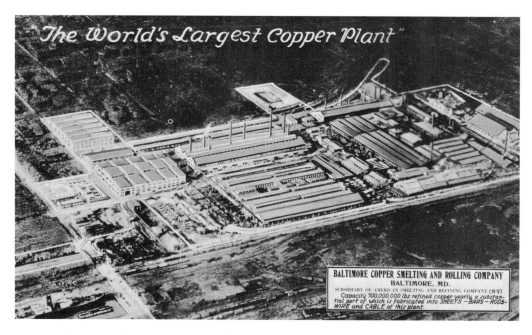

Baltimore Copper Smelting & Rolling Co., 1927

Company Handbook

Dr. Keener left the Baltimore and Cuba company in 1850 and with George Brown established the Baltimore Copper Smelting Company in Canton. He secured a good ore contract with Chilean producers and by 1860 the business was turning out 6,000,000 pounds of refined copper annually, the largest production in the United States. The operation was technically highly efficient and Keener's importation of a colony of Welsh smelters provided a trained work force which became self-perpetuating.

By 1864 the more efficient operation in Canton had convinced the owners of the Baltimore and Cuba Smelting and Mining Company across the river that they couldn't compete with Keener and the companies merged. Four years later the Locust Point property was sold and the Canton facility became the Baltimore Copper Company. Clinton Levering, ex-president of Baltimore and Cuba, was director of the new concern. Two prominent backers were Johns Hopkins and John W. Garrett.

At the same time the Gunpowder Copper Works founded by Hollingsworth was incorporated by Enoch Pratt, William Taylor, Galloway Cheston, Edward Clyme and William Pinckney. In 1883 the Gunpowder facility was abandoned and operations were transferred to a new, larger rolling mill next to the Baltimore Copper Company on Clinton Street. The Gunpowder works was renamed the Baltimore Copper Rolling Company. The president and secretary were Messrs. Pope and Cole. The situation was ripe for a final coalition.

Less than three years later, after the failure through outside investments of Pope, Cole and Company, the two copper concerns joined to form the Baltimore Copper Smelting and Rolling Company. By 1927 it was the largest copper refinery plant in the world.

The third most important factor in the early development of the port was importing raw materials to manufacture fertilizer. Maryland was one of the first states to make practical use of fertilizer on a large scale, and the port was the first major manufacturing and distribution center for the industry.

The arrival of the first cargo of Peruvian guano in Baltimore in 1832 may be regarded as the beginning of a new era in agriculture. Good fertilizer should contain three principal ingredients: nitrogen, which hastens the growth of plants; phosphates which stimulates root growth, and potash which aids starch formation and gives body to the plants. The use of Peruvian guano, containing much nitrogen and some potash, was a major step toward a satisfactory food for the soil, but it was not the final answer. The problem was solved when a German chemist treated bone and other substances containing lime with sulphuric acid to produce phosphoric acid, so essential to the quick growing of crops.

William Davison was born in South Ireland of well-to-do Scotch-Irish parents. When his family refused to sanction his marriage with the girl to whom he was engaged, the young man married her anyway, and emigrated to the United States, settling in Baltimore in 1826. A graduate of the University of Belfast, where he had specialized in chemistry, young Davison quite naturally turned to the subject with which he was most familiar. In 1832, in company with John Kettlewell, he built a plant in the Federal Hill area. This included what was probably the first sulphuric acid chamber in the United States.

From this beginning the industry developed. By 1880 there were 27 factories in the port, employing 2,500 persons. The aggregate product for that year was 280,000 tons of fertilizers, more than half the amount annually sold in the United States.

The raw materials used to manufacture these fertilizers were exceedingly varied, and came from all parts of the world. Phosphates from Spain, France, South Carolina; ground bone from Sicily; guano from Mexico, Peru and Navassa, an island

Coffee fleet at Fells Point

in the West Indies; nitrates from Chile and potash from Germany.

Raw materials were imported until the start of World War II. By then most of the fertilizer plants had moved to the Mid-West, closer to the bread basket of America. The port suffered a drastic reduction of import tonnage with phosphate rock being mined in Florida and new plants producing synthetic nitrates, plus the discovery of potash deposits in Canada and Southwest United States.

By the end of 1981 only three plants were manufacturing fertilizer in the port, and the only raw material being imported was an occasional cargo of potash from the Dead Sea Works in Israel.

Reese & Co.'s Guano Works

Enoch Pratt Free Library

COASTAL AND BAY TRADE—STEAMBOATING COMES TO AN END: 1825–1961

THE COASTAL TRADE, though not as important as the South American and European trades, nevertheless forms a significant portion of Baltimore's commerce.

Coastal shipping with the South had been carried on since Colonial times and it has been shown that commerce with the West Indies began as an extension of the coasting trade. By 1825 Baltimore was busy strengthening the latter by establishing a regular line of packets to Charleston, Savannah, and New Orleans. Trade did not stop here, however, but continued down along the Mexican coast. As early as 1829 Baltimore merchants were petitioning the President about the relative insecurity of that American trade.

From the Carolinas and Georgia, Baltimore received large quantities of timber, naval stores, cotton and rice, in return for whiskey, gin, corn, meats, flour, domestic and European goods. New Orleans shipped sugar, molasses, lead, cotton and salt meats from the Ohio Valley, in return for the best flour, and Baltimore and European manufactured products. Much of Baltimore's early extensive importation of linens was due to this trade with the South where the goods were found more durable and greatly prized.

As this trade increased—and with the advent of steam—new lines were established. In 1836 the Atlantic Steam Company ran two large steamers to Charleston and ordered the *Pulaski* built in a local shipyard. She was the largest of coast-wise steamers, but on her third trip from Savannah her boiler exploded through the negligence of an inexperienced engineer. The vessel broke in two and sank with a loss of 110 lives. This disaster, along with the breaking up of the Allaine steamer *Home,* shook the public confidence in coastal steamers to such an extent that not until 1846 did such lines become profitable.

While Baltimore had always enjoyed trade with other Chesapeake Bay ports, the introduction of steam led to its significant expansion. Sail-power on the Bay's many tributaries was, at best, tricky and rarely dependable, but steam provided both the needed reliability and ability to maneuver.

On both the Delaware River and waters around New York the commercial and engineering practicality of steam-propelled vessels had been demonstrated by 1810. After an investigation of those operations, the Union Line of Baltimore, led by Captain Edward Trippe, decided to try a steamer on the Bay. This was the *Chesapeake,* built by William Flanigan of Baltimore. After two exhibition trips, on June 21, 1813 she began regular runs to Frenchtown on the Elk River. The venture was immediately successful, almost driving the competing sailing packets out of business. From then on the history of steamboats on the Chesapeake was one of steady expansion of the

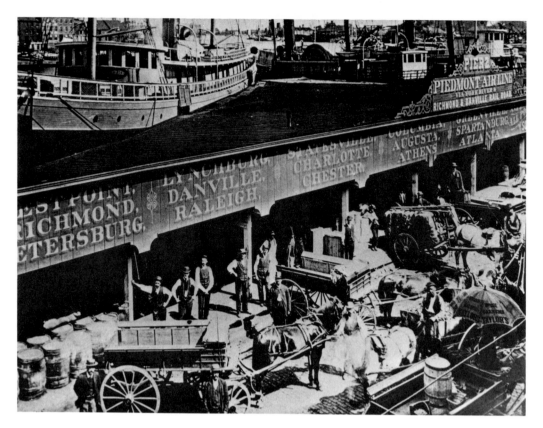

Pier 2, Light Street, about 1885

routes by small companies until every Bay or river port had both freight and passenger service to Baltimore, Washington or Norfolk.

New York carried on an extensive coastwise trade with Baltimore and the Chesapeake region. At an early period this reached such proportions that schooners were organized into packet lines. By 1836 five lines ran regularly to Baltimore. By 1849 regular lines of steam and sailing coasting vessels were plying from Baltimore to Boston, Providence, Hartford, New York, Norfolk, Richmond, Charleston, Savannah, New Orleans and the smaller ports.

The Merchants and Miners Transportation Company (then known as the Boston Steamship Company) was chartered in Maryland in 1852 and began service less than three years later with the yacht-like steamers *Joseph Whitney* and *William Jenkins*. The success of the line was so rapid that in 1859 the capital of the company was increased and two large new iron side-wheelers were added to the run. Thus began the greatest of all the coastal lines out of Baltimore, which, until World War II, carried the largest share of the port's coastwise trade.

For over a century the shipbuilding industry had been centered in the Fells Point area but when Charles Reeder, Sr. and John Watchman established plants in Federal Hill, new shipyards specializing in steamboats soon dotted those shores.

History must recognize Reeder and Watchman as the earliest pioneers in steamboat building in Baltimore. Their industry and vision were ultimately responsible for the impressive growth of shipbuilding in the port, which has continued to the present day. When these men began to install steam engines first in wooden hulls, later in iron, steampower itself was in its infancy. Much of their success was accomplished after repeated trials and sometimes disastrous failure, but their perserverance revolutionized their industry.

It was during this early period that the most fearsome disaster in the history of Chesapeake Bay steamboating occurred. The Brown and Collyer shipyard, at Federal Hill, had built the new steamer *Medora* for the Baltimore Steam Packet Company (Old Bay Line). John Watchman constructed and installed her engine and boiler at his wharf. On April 14, 1842, the *Medora* was in readiness for her trial trip. The numerous officials of the line and their invited guests, together with shipyard workers and crew, swelled the number on board to 79. After her lines were cast off, but before her engines had made two full revolutions, her boiler exploded. Her stack and the forward section of her upper deck, along with those standing there, were blown 40 feet into the air. The sides of the vessel around the boiler were blown to bits, and the iron boiler landed crosswise on the deck. The entire craft was enveloped in scalding steam, which killed several people; others were killed by flying timbers or drowned after being thrown or having jumped overboard. The vessel sank almost immediately.

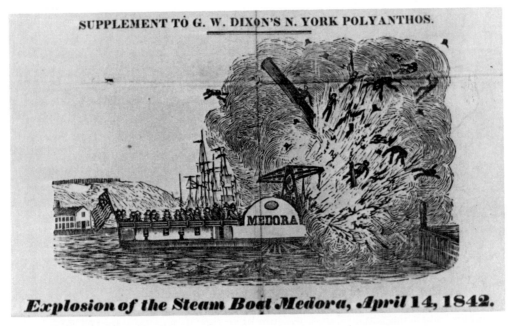

Explosion of the Steamboat Medora

Mariners Museum, Newport News, Va.

Gloom settled over the city as rescue workers, answering the plea of Mayor Solomon Hillen, began searching for the missing. At intervals, a cannon was fired over the basin in the belief that the concussion would cause the bodies to rise to the surface. Twenty-six persons, including Andrew F. Henderson, first president of the Old Bay Line, were killed and 38 were injured. Only fifteen escaped unhurt.

Steamboating on the Chesapeake can be divided into three primary divisions, the Eastern Shore, Western Shore, and the Baltimore-Norfolk route, the most important. The early Eastern Shore routes covered stops on the Chester, Miles,

Choptank, Wicomico and Nanticoke rivers in Maryland and the Pungoteague Creek in Virginia. The Western Shore routes included Annapolis and the West, Patuxent, Potomac Rivers in Maryland and the James, Rappahannock, York and Piankatank rivers in Virginia.

A FORT TO DEFEND THE PORT

In 1847 Sollers Flats, an island of four acres, lying between Sparrows and Hawkins Point, was transferred to the Federal government for the purpose of erecting a fort suitable for the defense of the city. Work commenced on March 1, 1848, under the command of Major Ogden, who had requested the building of the fort. On November 15 he was relieved by a brevet colonel of engineers. The relieving officer was a graduate of West Point and had seen action and meritorious service in the war with Mexico.

With his coming the new construction work was touched with future fame, for the old and abandoned fort known as Fort Carroll, is now referred to as the place where Baltimore first met a man destined to play a major part in American history, Robert E. Lee.

The original specifications called for a six-sided construction, with walls eight to ten feet thick, suitable to withstand shell fire for a protracted period. It was also to contain gun emplacements for 350 pieces of ordnance with sufficient ranging stations and watch towers. Within were to be ammunition arsenals, quarters for men and officers, as well as adequate water supplies.

For the next three years Colonel Lee lived with his family at 908 Madison Avenue, a three-story brick row house across the street from Mt. Calvary Church, near Hamilton Terrace. It was a happy period for him; he had relatives in Baltimore and enjoyed a pleasant social life.

In 1850, "the Fort at Sollers Point Flats" was given its present name for Charles Carroll of Carrollton, who before his death at 95, in 1832, had been the last surviving signer of the Declaration of Independence.

At the end of four years the War Department had partially lost interest in the project, and appropriations were made more and more slowly. Then Colonel Lee was ordered to West Point to become the Military Academy's ninth superintendent.

In 1852 Congress failed to appropriate new funds for the fort and under Lee's successors, work lagged. A ring of gun embrasures was completed, with brick magazines, storerooms and troop quarters; but the entire structure was found to be settling, and work stopped. Eventually, even the settling stopped.

During the Spanish-American War and World War I, batteries of guns ranging from 2-inch to 12-inch were installed. A company came over from Fort McHenry every day except Sunday to practice. During World War II the Coast Guard used it as a pistol range, and seamen were housed there while their ships were being fumigated.

In 1942 a salvage expedition collected 100 tons of iron scrap for use in munitions. This included a crane on the landing dock and a flag tower. Newspapers jested that the old fort, never used for defense, now was to share in the Allied offense.

The fort has held a succession of lighthouses, one of them automatic, all found to be unneeded.

Fort Carroll

A. Aubrey Bodine

For more than a century, Baltimoreans have been trying to find other uses for the island, which has had only one permanent resident, the lighthouse tender who also cranked a fog bell by hand every two hours. He left in 1920. The first recorded suggestion came from Mayor Mahool in 1909. It was to erect a large statue of Cecilius Calvert. It was also suggested as site for the huge statue of Orpheus, now at Fort McHenry. In 1955 Governor McKeldin offered the island to the city. Mayor D'Alesandro politely refused.

In 1958 Benjamin N. Eisenberg, a Baltimore attorney, bought Fort Carroll from the Federal Government for $10,100. He planned to develop the island as park, museum and restaurant. The cost of restoring the fort was estimated at more than $250,000. A dispute arose as to whether the island was in Baltimore or Anne Arundel County. Baltimore County fired the first shot in the battle for jurisdiction when it assessed the acreage at $34,500 and the fort at $15,500. Mr. Eisenberg claimed it was south of the original harbor channel and thus in Anne Arundel County. For the next two years the Battle of Fort Carroll was fought in the tax courts until Mr. Eisenberg decided to give up the fight and discontinue the project.

Having fallen into a desolation almost picturesque, but mysteriously alluring, the fort appears to have reached its low point. Given a strange, timeless beauty by its emptiness, the fort, which has a ghostlike air, is in startling contrast to the busy port on all sides.

The Port—Pride of Baltimore / 43

STEAMBOATING ON THE BAY

During the middle 1930s the steamboats on the Bay began to fall victim to an expanding highway system carrying ever-increasing numbers of trucks and automobiles. On July 29, 1937 a disaster occurred which helped doom steamboating on the Bay.

That evening the *City of Baltimore* of the Chesapeake Steamship Company sailed from her Light Street pier bound for Norfolk with a full complement of passengers and freight. As she passed North Port entering the Bay the cry of "Fire!" was sounded. The Captain steered the steamer out of the channel toward land until it hit a sand bank. Within minutes flames were shooting out of the forward section and working aft. Passengers and crew began to leap overboard. Fortunately the *State of Maryland, Wm. D. Sanner* and the *Maryland* were nearby, rushed to the scene and launched lifeboats. The heat was so intense that the rescue craft were forced to keep some distance from the blazing vessel. By the light of the roaring fire they hauled the exhausted swimmers to safety. By midnight the *City of Baltimore* had burned down to the metal hull leaving only her stack and boiler casing standing. Two persons were known dead and two missing, out of the 90 on board.

At that time the Western Shore Steamboat Company was the only small steamboat line carrying passengers and freight from Baltimore to various stops on the Bay. Steamboat inspectors reported to the company that to obtain a renewal of its certificate to carry passengers and pass future inspections, it would be necessary to install fireproof bulkheads in the metal hull of its steamer and an automatic

The Anne Arundel docks at St. Marys City, 1936   *A. Aubrey Bodine*

sprinkler system. The officials decided that with poor business prospects they had little hope of recouping those costs so the company went out of business.

This ended that phase of steamboating represented by the smaller side-wheelers and propellers that threaded the Chesapeake and its tributaries for over a century. The Chesapeake Bay Steamship Line and the Baltimore Steam Packet Company (The Old Bay Line) continued to operate their large steamboats to Norfolk.

For over 122 years the Old Bay Line formed an important segment of the port's economy, but it also fell victim to increased truck traffic, strikes and the high cost of replacing aging vessels.

The Old Bay Line was organized in 1840 by some of the board of directors of the Maryland Virginia Steamboat Company which ceased operations in 1839. It survived three wars, but not without complications. During the Civil War the Norfolk Terminal fell to the Confederates forcing the company to move its southern terminal to Old Point Comfort. On January 1, 1918, the U.S. Government took over the management of all railroads and steamboat lines and combined the operation of the Old Bay Line and the Chesapeake Steamship Company for the duration of the war.

In 1941 the Old Bay Line absorbed the Chesapeake Steamship Company, which marked the end of a competing service to Norfolk that began in 1896.

World War II was different. In 1942 due to the heavy shipping losses suffered by England, the War Shipping Administration acquired from the Old Bay Line the steamers *President Warfield* and *Yorktown* and transferred them to the British Ministry. They were in convoy RB-1 which left St. Johns, Newfoundland, on September 21, 1942. Five days later they were attacked by German submarines and the *Yorktown* was sunk. The *Warfield,* by quick helm action, managed to maneuver to let a torpedo pass 30 feet away. The convoy dispersed and the *Warfield* finally reached an Irish seaport.

The next few months of the *Warfield's* career were uneventfully spent at moorings off the little English town of Instow on the Torridge River where, fast in the mud at low tide, she served as a Combined Operations training and barracks ship. The United States Navy took her back from the British in July, 1943 and she became *U.S.S. President Warfield (IS 169).* She then began her pre-Normandy invasion role of an assault boat training base. In April, 1944 she moved on to Barry Roads and in the comparative calm of D-plus-30 day, she crossed the Channel to Omaha Beach where she served as a station and accommodation ship for harbor control. She went back to the United Kingdom in November, 1944. After a stretch of temporary duty running on the Seine, she ultimately recrossed the Atlantic to Hampton Roads where she was berthed at the Naval Operations Base at Norfolk, being decommissioned and offered for sale by the Maritime Commission on September 19, 1945. She was then towed up the James to the idle fleet anchorage to await a prospective purchaser. Her former owners did not want her because of the major and expensive overhaul necessary to reconvert her to their passenger service. She was accordingly sold on an unrestricted basis to the Potomac Shipwrecking Company of Washington for $8,028.

It is said that this company turned a tidy profit by selling her two days later for $40,000 to a concern that called itself the Western Trading Company of New York, a front for Haganah, a Palestine underground organization. It later developed that the ship had been paid for by sympathizers of the Zionist movement in Baltimore.

Including the purchase price, it was reported that between $125,000 and $130,000 were spent on outfitting and repairs. Around the Baltimore waterfront the first rumors were that *President Warfield* was bound for China. Flying the flag of Honduras, in whose registry she had been enrolled, she headed down the Patapsco

River in mid-February 1947. Again eastbound across the Atlantic, *President Warfield* ran into heavy weather 75 miles east of Diamond Shoals and started some seams. Leaking badly, the ship radioed distress signals, the tanker *H.C. Sinclair* stood by, and the Coast Guard sent the cutter *Cherokee* to assist the steamer it had once fired on. Damage and flooding were restricted to the forehold, and once the weather moderated the ship was able to steam back to Norfolk, with a slight list and down by the head, but still at good speed. This unwelcomed spotlight increased the mystery surrounding her attempted departure. Unexpectedly returned to port, it was discovered that most of the crew were Jewish and that the cargo consisted merely of 25 tons of life preservers and mess kits. Captain William S. Schlegel said he knew nothing of the ship's ultimate destiny and that by his orders he had only planned to deliver her to Marseilles.

President Warfield, 1928

Steamship Historical Society Collection

Again patched up, and with a new skipper, *President Warfield* slipped away two weeks later and this time she made it across the Atlantic. Jewish immigrants secretly boarded her at the French port of Sette in early July and the now heavily-laden destroyer, which had been shadowing the *Warfield* pulled alongside and inquired if any illegal immigrants for Palestine were on board. Since there were some 4,500 of them and the steamer was almost literally bursting at the seams, this question was obviously rhetorical. But it was posed again on the next day and on the day following, but always ignored by the *Warfield's* company, who elected to answer by playing "Pomp and Circumstance" over the public address system. By the sixth day, with the territorial waters of Palestine just under the horizon, the *Warfield's* unwanted escort had been augmented by *H. M. Cruiser Ajax*, five destroyers and two mine-sweepers. A final plea from *Ajax* to give up was unheeded.

Early on the eighth day two destroyers closed not too gently on either side of the *Warfield*. Repelled at first by a spirited defense of tin cans, sticks and potatoes, the British boarders cleared the decks with tear gas and jumped aboard. With a gash on her port side, the Royal Navy convoyed her submissively into Haifa and her passengers were transferred to three 'prison ships' for the long and sad retracing of the fruitless journey which terminated at Hamburg on September 7, 1947, some two months after their "odyssey of frustration" had begun.

The *Warfield* lay at Haifa until August 26, 1952, when she caught fire and burned. Her remains were sold for scrap, thus ending the exceptional career of this Chesapeake Bay steamboat.

For over a decade after the war, the Old Bay Line continued to handle freight and passengers on a daily basis but the future became dark. In November, 1959, the U.S. Army Engineers condemned the Old Point Comfort pier and ordered it dismantled. Due to the rising cost of labor, the Old Bay Line discontinued carrying passengers on Labor Day, 1961. For the next eight months the line continued hauling cargo, but faced with threatened strikes and the rapid deterioration of the aging steamers, the Old Bay Line finally ended operations on April 13, 1962.

The Old Bay Line song was published in 1922, the music by George Graff, Jr., who also wrote "When Irish Eyes are Smiling."

The City of Norfolk, Old Bay Line, entering Baltimore Harbor.   *A. Aubrey Bodine*

First two verses

"Come take a trip on the Bay Line's ships
On the steamship *Florida*
It leaves every day Norfolk VA
Or else from Baltimore.

"You take a trip on the Bay Line's ships
You enjoy every minute too
To sail away along the bay
It thrills you thru and thru."

What was more relaxing than taking a trip on an Old Bay Line steamer? One would arrive at the pier around 4:30 PM, have an attendant take your baggage while your car was loaded aboard. You would go to the upper deck and watch freight being loaded until the familiar call, "All ashore that's going ashore." The steamer would slowly back away from the pier and start the delightful trip down the Bay. You could relax in a deck chair and watch the sights of the busy harbor until the dinner call was sounded. The dining saloon was immaculate and served traditional Maryland dishes and all types of seafood. The costs of the meals were reasonable; as late as 1960, the dinners were about $2.00. After dinner, strolling the deck, you could be captivated on moonlight nights by the moon's reflection on the water and fascinated by the flickering shore lights. You could then retire to your stateroom and be lulled to sleep by the gentle roll of the steamer. By the time you had finished breakfast the next morning the steamer had docked and your car was waiting at the gangway. All this for $10.00 a round trip, plus $6.65 each way for the best stateroom.

The chorus

"Sailing, sailing no matter which way
Sailing upward or down the bay
On the good *Alabama* you sure do have fun
And the *Florida* too, for those boats they can run."
"Sailing, sailing you have to feel gay
And the crew will I'll say they sure know their way
So be sure when you come to bring some good chum
And I know you will have fun."

The thousands of students and teachers who took a trip during spring vacations and the businessmen who used the Old Bay Line to break a daily routine would certainly agree with those words and so would the many families who used the line enroute to a vacation at Virginia Beach or a visit to Williamsburg.

When the Old Bay Line stopped operating a great Maryland-Virginia tradition of steamboating was lost. The Chesapeake Bay with its many rivers, creeks and coves, is considered the most beautiful inland waterway in the United States. For over a hundred and twenty years the Old Bay Line gave its passengers the opportunity to observe and enjoy those beauties.

THE CIVIL WAR AND ITS AFTERMATH: 1861–1891

THE EVENTS WHICH followed the election of President Lincoln, the secession of South Carolina and the Gulf states, the growing animosity on both sides, and the ineffectual efforts to bring about a peaceful settlement, were watched in Baltimore with intense interest. Most Baltimoreans sympathized with the South, but only a few wanted Maryland to secede; devotion to the Union under the Constitution was the majority's sentiment. As ideologies clashed, however, the division of sympathies became more pronounced, and men began to side with the North or South.

At a late hour on Friday, April 12, 1861, a dispatch from Charleston, S.C. announced that the attack on Fort Sumter had begun.

On the waterfront the situation was most acute. The palmetto flag was not permitted to fly in the harbor. The display of a secession flag from the mizzen topmast of the barque *Fanny Crenshaw* caused a near riot on the 14th. Four days later a mob of Southern supporters gleefully ascended Federal Hill with a flagpole, a Confederate flag, and a cannon. They hoisted the flag and began firing a salute. Union supporters stormed the hill, driving the rebel sympathizers off. The rebel flag was burned and the cannon rolled into the basin.

The next day—one of the darkest days in the history of Baltimore—a 35-car trainload of troops, the Sixth Massachusetts regiment, arrived at the President Street Station at the eastern end of town.

They were armed, but somehow, instead of forming to march to Camden Station, one mile west, the men were kept in their cars for a horse-drawn trip along rails, the conventional route for civilians. A few cars got through, scarred with a fusillade of stones.

About one-third of the way along their path, derisive, disorderly crowds blocked the car route with sand, anchors and stones pulled off the docks near Gay and Pratt streets. The showered troops reformed on foot for the march to Camden Station. Stones were hurled and the angry crowd turned into a mob of pistol-wielding insurgents. The New Englanders fired a volley and then another and the line of march became a running fight between citizens and soldiers.

Baltimore's mayor, mild-spirited George William Brown, rushed from Camden Station to help quell the trouble along Pratt Street, but things were too far gone. Citizens, soldiers were falling on both sides. They were dragged into storefronts for emergency care or rescued from the mob by fellow soldiers.

Somehow, most of the sorely tried regiment made it to Camden Station and boarded for Washington. Four soldiers and eleven citizens were killed in the riot.

News of the violence inspired James Ryder Randall, a Baltimorean who was then living in New Orleans, to write the stirring song, "Maryland, My Maryland."

Federal Hill, 1863   *Enoch Pratt Free Library*

The north began to assail Baltimore through its press. An editorial in the New York *Tribune* read:

> "One section of the country is only semi-civilized in a society so constituted it is not strange that there should be found many persons who could conceive and execute some diabolical plot of slaughter."

In Boston, incensed by the attack on the Sixth Massachusetts Infantry, the natives began to sing:

> "There's swelling cry for vengeance on the counterfeits of men who haunt that hold of pirates—that foul assassin's den!"

On May 13, 1861, a regiment of Union soldiers under the command of General Benjamin F. Butler left Relay marching to Baltimore to occupy Federal Hill. Butler wrote a proclamation to be published in the local newspapers. He began by saying, "A detachment of forces of the Federal government under my command have occupied the City of Baltimore, for the purpose, among other things, of enforcing respect and obedience to laws." He banned the display of any secession flags or banners, and directed all state military officers to report to him. Under his direction his men hastily constructed fortifications and gun emplacements on Federal Hill. General Butler directed his largest cannon at the Maryland Club on Monument Square, known to be the hotbed of Rebel dissidence, and issued the following order to his artillery commander: "If I am attacked, please open on Monument Square with your mortars."

The Mayor of Baltimore, fearing more bloodshed, destroyed the bridges of the Northern Central and the Philadelphia, Wilmington and Baltimore railroads, north of the city, thus cutting off Baltimore. The Baltimore and Ohio Railroad, which served the port from the west, was immobilized by the raids of the Confederate calvary.

When the Baltimore links with the north and west were broken, trade halted.

The Confederacy knew that Baltimore, with its large warehouses and wharves, was a natural depot for the Union armies in Virginia. The South was so anxious to win Maryland over to its side that it favored the Baltimore ships when captured by Confederate privateers. Out of the hundreds of ships seized or destroyed by the raiders, only ten had cleared from or were bound to Baltimore.

During the first three years of the war the port suffered immeasurably. The military authorities enforced an embargo which almost eliminated the coffee and flour trade. Wharves and warehouses were barren, and shipyards lay idle. The merchants of Baltimore were forced to import or export their goods through one of the northern ports.

In the fall of 1863 conditions improved slightly as several Union expeditions were outfitted for operations against the South. A few shipyards were re-activated when a number of U.S. naval vessels were sent to Baltimore for repairs and refitting. Some of the major repair jobs reported by *The Sun* were the *George Peabody* which had collided with the *West Point* and the *Louisiana,* which had collided with and sunk the Government steamer *Cambria.* Another was the *Adelaide,* which had accidentally run on the sunken wreck of the Confederate ironclad *Merrimac,* sometime after the latter's engagement with the Union ironclad *Monitor,* also the *Planter* of the Weems Line, a company whose owners were known as Confederate sympathizers.

Baltimore and the port were naturally central to the development of innumerable Civil War intelligence operations and plots; but for sheer audacity and intrigue, the "French Lady Affair" stands out.

The event was the capture of the *St. Nicholas,* a side-wheeler which plied from Baltimore, via St. Mary's and Charles counties, to Georgetown, D.C. Undoubtedly, the star of the show, which at times verged on farce, was the 28-year-old Richard Thomas.

He was born into an old and illustrious Maryland family in 1833 in St. Mary's county. His father was Richard Thomas, a Speaker of the House of Delegates, a large slave holder and a staunch Southern sympathizer. Thomas was educated at Charlotte Hall, and for a short time was a cadet at the U.S. Military Academy. Later he was a surveyor on the Western frontier, then a soldier of fortune in the Far East where he fought Chinese pirates. Eventually he landed in Europe and joined Garibaldi's forces then struggling for independence in Italy. It was in Italy that he adopted what could be termed a 'stage name,' "Zarvona." Shortly before the outbreak of the Civil War, he returned to America to aid the Confederates.

There was controversy about who masterminded the plot to capture the *St. Nicholas:* Captain George Hollins, Lieutenant H. H. Lewis and Richard Thomas all claimed credit. Certainly Thomas possessed the imagination and audacity. Charles Earp in *"The Amazing Colonel Zarvona"* gives this account of the plot:

"It was proposed to secrete a band of carefully disguised volunteers on board the *Saint Nicholas,* overpower her crew at a strategic moment and take command of the vessel. Then by a quick trip to the Coan (sic) River on the Virginia shore the little force was to be augmented by a detachment of the Confederate infantry. The *Saint Nicholas,* it appears, frequently transferred supplies to the United States warship *Pawnee,* a vessel of the Federal squadron which patrolled the Chesapeake Bay. Consequently the final step in the plan was to range alongside the *Pawnee* as usual, throw an armed force on board and capture the vessel for the Confederacy by a surprise stroke before the Federals became aware of the ruse."

Governor Letcher of Virginia, entrusted Thomas with $1,000 to purchase arms and supplies in Philadelphia. Once this had been accomplished, Thomas arrived in Baltimore and joined his volunteers.

On June 28, 1861, the *St. Nicholas* set out on her normal run to Georgetown. Among the passengers in Baltimore was a "French Lady," a "Madame Zarvona" no doubt, who embarked with several milliner's trunks. The "dark, masculine-featured lady" was, of course, none other than Richard Thomas. The *St. Nicholas* proceeded to Point Lookout, making her scheduled stops along the way, unknowingly collecting clandestine conspirators intermingled with legitimate passengers. At Point Lookout two additional pseudo-passengers were taken aboard: Captain Hollins and Lieutenant Alexander. The latter recalled that he spotted Thomas rendering an impeccable performance as the "French Lady," fluttering her fan while engaged in animated coquettish conversation with an enthralled Federal officer, oblivious of the impersonation. After the steamer cleared port, the enticing Zarvona made her excuses and retired. Doffing his curls and petticoats he donned the uniform of a Confederate Zouave, appeared with a cutlass in one hand and pistol in the other. The volunteers rushed to his stateroom, seized their weapons from the milliner's trunks and overpowered the passengers and crew. As planned, Capt. Hollins assumed command and set off for the rendezvous with Lt. Lewis on the Cone River. The proposed attack on the *Pawnee* had to be abandoned but Captain Hollins was keen to reap other spoils from their venture so the *St. Nicholas* proceeded out to the Bay and captured three vessels. The first was the *Monticello*, bound for Baltimore from Brazil, carrying 3,500 bags of coffee. Next the *Mary Pierce* was taken on her way to Washington from Boston, loaded with 260 tons of ice, much needed in Confederate hospitals. Lastly, the capture of the *Margaret* proved to be most auspicious as she was carrying 270 tons of coal when the *St. Nicholas* had amost exhausted its supply.

On July 1, Governor Letcher commissioned Richard Thomas Zarvona, as an officer in the Confederate Navy. He soon set off for Baltimore to try to duplicate his previous success. This proved foolhardy as his exploits had become well known and Federal troops were determined to arrest him.

Sailing from Fair Haven, Maryland to Baltimore on the *Mary Washington* he was recognized by several who had been aboard the *St. Nicholas*. They informed two members of the Baltimore police force who were aboard and ordered the steamer to Fort McHenry. "Zarvona" came forward and challenged the policemen's authority, drew a pistol, and threatened to throw one overboard, but he was outnumbered. When the *Mary Washington* reached Fort McHenry, all were ordered ashore—all except the elusive "Zarvona" who had miraculously disappeared. After an hour-and-a-half search by a company of infantry he was discovered hidden in a lady's cabin. He was confined in Fort McHenry for several months and then transferred to Fort Lafayette in New York harbor. There he attempted an audacious escape. Although he could not swim, he sought to reach the Long Island shore by keeping afloat with corked tin cans dangling from his belt. His disappearance was quickly noticed and a boat was sent to retrieve him. Finally, through the intercession of Governor Letcher of Virginia and members of Congress, he was released in April, 1863, never having been tried. He returned to Europe where he lived in Paris for some years. He died in Southern Maryland in 1875.

Had the bold, brazen plan of a young Confederate naval officer been successful, it would have been one of the most daring feats of the Civil War.

Charles W. Read of Mississippi was a second lieutenant on the Confederate privateer *Florida* under the command of Captain Maffitt. On May 6, 1863 the *Florida* captured the *Clarence* bound for Brown's Wharf in Baltimore with a cargo of Brazilian coffee. A few hours after the capture, Lt. Read presented the following letter to Captain Maffitt:

"Sir: I propose to take the brig which we have just captured, and with a crew of 20 men to proceed to Hampton Roads and cut out a gunboat or steamer of the enemy. As I would be in possession of the Brig's papers, and as the crew would be not large enough to excite suspicion, there can be no doubt of my passing Fortress Monroe successfully. Once in the Roads I would prepare to avail myself of any circumstances which might present for gaining the check of an enemy's vessel. If it was found impossible to board a gunboat or merchant steamers, it would be possible to fire the shipping at Baltimore."

Very respectfully, your obedient servant
C. W. Read, Second Lieutenant, C.S. Navy

Captain Maffitt was intrigued by the idea and had the *Clarence* outfitted for him. After taking command, the young officer made the ship more formidable, in appearance at least, by adding several wooden guns. The *Clarence* captured a number of federal merchant ships as it made its way north to the Chesapeake Bay. From a northern newspaper found aboard one of the prizes, Lt. Read learned that the security at Hampton Roads was so strict that only a Union transport carrying government goods could get through. He decided to cruise along the coast to try to capture a transport and "in the meantime do all possible damage to the enemy commerce." When Read was captured on June 24, after he had destroyed 21 Union merchant ships, his plan for burning the shipping in Baltimore was still only a dream.

As soon as the war ended on April 9, 1865, there was a wide-spread agitation to re-establish commercial relations with the South. Such trade had been an important part of the city's commerce before the war, and it was necessary that it be restored if Baltimore were to keep pace with her northern rivals.

Businessmen agreed that Baltimore should take the lead, as far as possible, in granting loans to enable southern houses to recover, and in fostering a revival of trade with the Virginia cities in particular. This attitude was the result of sentimental ties, close personal and business connections, but principally of cold economic reasoning that the sooner the South recovered, the sooner it could afford to buy Baltimore merchandise. Throughout the reconstruction period, and the succeeding years, Baltimore labored to restore her southern trade to its former level.

Charles W. Gold, a veteran of the Civil War, and a Captain B. D. Riddell of the 4th Maryland Infantry, both Baltimoreans, conceived an unusual and what became a fateful voyage across the Atlantic. Their craft was a double-ender 24 feet 6 inches in length with a 7-foot beam. While it was under construction Captain Gold's funds ran out, but John T. Ford of Baltimore and a few of his friends came to his aid. When the boat was completed at a reported cost of $1,200, she was named after Mr. Ford.

When questioned about the purpose of the trip, Captain Gold said he wanted "to prove to the people of Europe that the American sailor is as likely to be afloat on a bundle of shingles as in a 2,000 ton ship." The *John T. Ford* measured only 2.35 tons. The plan was to exhibit the vessel at the Paris Exposition in the belief that the dare devil voyage would make her an object of commercial interest.

On June 22, 1867, she started down the Patapsco River in tow of the city tug *Baltimore* as thousands of spectators cheered. She had been supplied with hermetically sealed provisions and enough water to enable her crew to reach Europe in the captain's predicted time of 35 days. Her crew consisted of Captain Gold, Captain Riddle, John Shaney and 16-year-old Edward Murphy. In passing the wharves of the Cuba Steamship Company a two-gun salute was fired and answered by cheers from the tug and the *Ford*.

Start of fateful ocean voyage of the tiny John T. Ford, center, to right of three row boats
Enoch Pratt Free Library

Passing out of the Virginia capes the *Ford* sailed up the coast arriving in Halifax, Nova Scotia on July 16. Captain Riddle left, as she had shown herself too small in his opinion to carry four persons across the Atlantic. He was replaced by Andrew Armstrong. After minor repairs the *Ford* sailed from Halifax on July 16.

On the afternoon of August 5, while carrying all sails, she was struck by a heavy sea and overturned. She righted almost immediately but the oil supply for cooking and lighting the binnacle lamp was lost along with her fresh water. Unable to cook their food, and lacking drinking water, the men became ill. For fuel they cut up the interior joiner work and the boards which kept the ballast in place. On two occasions they might have been saved by passing vessels, but they only asked for provisions.

On August 18 the *Ford* reached the entrance to the English Channel where she ran into a sudden squall which capsized the vessel. The loose ballast shifted and was thrown overboard. The men tried to cling to the overturned wreck but were swept off repeatedly.

By August 23, Armstrong was the only survivor. That day the *Aerolite,* outbound from Liverpool, sighted a piece of canvas attached to an oar on the *Ford* and sailed down to investigate. Armstrong was rescued, exhausted and insensible. The next day he was transferred to the *Mary Blake,* which took him to London where he was cared for by the American consul.

The *John T. Ford* remained afloat and on September 6 was washed ashore at Tacumshane, on the Wexford coast of Ireland. Without a crew she had completed the passage, with an assist from the currents and winds. Thus was the end of a foolhardy venture from which no practical good would have been possible even if it had been successful.

On October 30, 1865, George S. Brown, president of Alex Brown & Sons, organized a company to establish a coastwise steamship line from Baltimore to Charleston and Havana. Capital was quickly acquired and a fleet of steamers built. In December the first vessel sailed from Brown's Wharf in Fells Point with a full cargo. The company was so successful that in three years New Orleans was added to the route. Due to the success of this small company other lines of steamers were soon established with the South. The Richmond and York River Line, operating from Baltimore, opened branch lines on the James and Potomac rivers, and through the North Carolina sounds to New Bern and Wilmington. The northern-sponsored Leary Line entered the competition on the Norfolk run, soon followed by the Baltimore, Chesapeake and Richmond Steamship Company. In addition, the Merchants and Miners extended its line once more to Savannah.

To one who had spent the prime of his life in the antebellum city and had known the princes of the Thirties and Forties, Baltimore had changed greatly in four years of war. "Rebellion has vitiated the atmosphere of the marketplace, and flaunts its symbols on the streets. Old friends keep apart, pass with unpleasant glances or converse together without a topic or with strange constraint," wrote the venerable John Pendleton Kennedy. But this was not all. To the old statesman, the "vigor of mental activity" which had been such an important factor in the unprecedented growth of the port had been lost. The city was now "careworn and contentious, unpleasantly characterized by a struggle between generosity and selfishness. Cloven by faction." One man, however, had not lost the spirit of enterprise in the days when Baltimore boldly set out to conquer the West by railroad. This was John W. Garrett, president of the B & O Railroad.

Mr. Garrett was convinced the port needed a transatlantic steamship line. With the approval of his company he purchased three wooden screw ships from the Federal government which had been used as blockaders during the war. After repairs and alterations, they were named the *Worcester, Carroll* and *Somerset.* They were small brig-rigged and had limited passenger accommodations. The *Worcester,* the largest, was 218 feet long, 1,500 gross tons, and had a speed of ten knots.

Fells Point was buzzing with excitement as the day of the inauguration of the line approached. On September 29, 1865 *The Sun* reported:

"The steamship, *Somerset,* one of the vessels about to be inaugurated between this port and Liverpool, and which has been undergoing extensive repairs and alterations, is now so far completed as to be able to start on her first trip across the ocean, as the pioneer of the enterprise, the success of which is of such importance to the mercantile interest of Baltimore. In addition to the elaborate work put upon the hull of the vessel, Messrs. Jas. Clark & Co. of the People's Machine & Boiler Works, have placed a new shaft in her and her engines have

John W. Garrett   *Baltimore Sunpapers*

been thoroughly overhauled and refitted. A brief trial trip of the *Somerset* was made a few days since, when a number of gentlemen interested in the enterprise were on board, and after running some 16 miles expressed themselves perfectly satisfied with the ship in every respect. With 15 pounds of steam she made 35 revolutions per minute, and it was asserted that she can make ten knots with 25 pounds of steam, her usual standard. At noon tomorrow, the *Somerset* leaves this port for Liverpool. She will start from Henderson's Wharf, foot of Fell Street. All her cargo is aboard, several persons are booked as passengers. The cargo is nearly as follows: 300 bales of cotton, 100 hogsheads of tobacco, 6,000 bushels of corn, 800 sacks oilcake, 40 tons bark, a large quantity of dye-stuffs, canned fruits and miscellaneous articles. During yesterday about 50 shipjoiners and painters were at work in her, and with this force, by Saturday the repairs and alterations will be completed.

"At and around Henderson's Wharf there will be ample room for many persons to congregate at the time of the departure of the vessel, the occasion being one of which Baltimoreans may be truly proud. As the ship leaves the wharf she will be saluted from Fort Federal Hill and by the U.S. revenue cutter, and will also be saluted as she passes Fort McHenry. These salutes will be returned by the *Somerset*. The U.S. revenue cutter will convey a large party of ladies and gentlemen some distance down the Bay. Among these will be Major Gen. Hancock, Hon. Thomas Swann, Governor-elect, Mayor Chapman, John W. Garrett, Esq., and other distinguished gentlemen. It is understood that a steamboat will leave the adjoining wharf, and accompany the *Somerset* as far as North Point, on board of which persons can take a short excursion and witness the departure of the pioneer ship of this ocean line between Baltimore and Liverpool."

The next morning thousands of spectators along the shores of Fells Point cheered as the *Somerset* left on her maiden voyage. The excitement did not die down until the *Somerset* returned and the *Worcester* had sailed on her maiden voyage. At last, regular steam transportation with Europe had been achieved.

But it was soon apparent that the three vessels were unable to compete successfully with foreign lines. After three years of operation they were withdrawn and the line suspended. Nevertheless, these staunch ships had inaugurated a new era for the port. And they had the distinction of being the only steamers on the Atlantic to fly the American flag for more than three years after the Civil War—so depleted had the American merchant marine become. Before they were withdrawn, however, a more important service was organized.

Sailing of the steamer Somerset from Baltimore

Peale Museum

On January 21, 1867 Mr. Garrett signed an agreement with the North German Lloyd Steamship Company to run at least two first-class iron steamers between Baltimore and Bremen for five years or more. The line had been highly successful in New York and was thoroughly experienced in operating ships on a large scale. Service opened with the arrival of the *Baltimore* on March 24, 1868, from Bremen with a heavy cargo and full complement of passengers, to the intense excitement of the city. The line proved such an immediate success that two more ships were built and the capital doubled. When the new stock was offered the merchants of Bremen were so eager to share in the profits that they offered over 40 times the desired subscription.

The wharves in Fells Point were too small to accommodate the new steamers so Garrett decided to develop Locust Point as a modern deepwater terminal. There, on the Northwest Branch of the Patapsco, at the gateway of the deep inner harbor

Rail yards and docks, Locust Point

Maryland Historical Society

with abundant fairway to manipulate the largest ship, he erected a large dock and grain elevator system. Large piers with rail sidings alongside were constructed so cargoes could be handled directly to or from rail cars. Two grain elevators were built with a combined capacity of over 2,000,000 bushels. It was not, however, until 1873 that both elevators were completed. In that year, the grain exportation at Locust Point, which five years before had been negligible, reached a total of 7,251,717 bushels. Other special warehouse facilities were devised for the handling of sugar and coffee. But the great strength of Locust Point in those days was in the export coal traffic. The new coal loading facility was always well filled with vessels taking aboard coal, either as cargo or as fuel.

Meanwhile, the B & O Railroad was pushing west, reaching Chicago in 1874 and connecting Baltimore with the great lines in the Middle West. The Northern Central Railway gave access to the coal fields of Pennsylvania and the ports of the Great Lakes. The Western Maryland Railway was beginning to develop the western portion of the state. Baltimore was now connected with three large trunk lines.

By 1868 New York was becoming anxious at the diversion of trade to Baltimore, particularly because of its lower freight rates. On April 11 the Baltimore *Gazette* listed these freight charges from New York and Baltimore to different parts of the West for fourth class goods. They foreshadow the great rate-differential struggle which would begin in 1877 and continue to the present.

To	From New York	From Baltimore
	cents per hundred	
Cincinnati	50	30
Louisville	66	48
St. Louis	94	55
Chicago	55	38
Indianapolis	53	35

In 1827 the founder of the Baltimore & Ohio Railroad had foreseen Baltimore's advantage in her proximity to the West. Fifty years later that advantage was clearly revealed in the comparative railroad distances from various points in the West.

From	To Baltimore	To New York
Chicago	767	890
Cleveland	444	562
Louisville	688	852
Pittsburgh	313	436
St. Louis	891	1040

The rate differential, more than anything else, governs the volume of tonnage moving to and from the port and the general character of the port's commerce. The rate wars which accompanied railroad expansion after the war need hardly be mentioned. By 1876 railroads were facing bankruptcy. Naturally, the northern trunk lines fought to abolish the differential, just as the B & O and the Northern Central (later the Pennsylvania Railroad) desired to keep it. To prevent more open warfare and to settle the dispute, the northeastern railroads formed the Trunk Line Association. The result was the momentous Differential Rate Agreement of April 5, 1877, the cornerstone of the Atlantic Port differentials of future years. The agreement was a compromise between the two demands—that rates be based on cost and that they be based on distance. A basis of percentage was established to be effective in all the territory under the jurisdiction of the Association, with Baltimore and Philadelphia given favorable differentials.

A great impetus to the development of the port was the construction of the Union Railroad, a Canton Company enterprise, to provide railroad facilities for the growing Canton industries. The project had been proposed in 1854, but had been repeatedly blocked by political opposition. In 1866 the Union Railroad Company of Baltimore was chartered by the Maryland Legislature. Work commenced in 1867, but was suspended in 1868. In 1870 the Canton Company subscribed for all the company's stock, and endorsed $900,000 of its bonds. The company endeavored to overcome partisan opposition by inviting all the Baltimore railroads to join the enterprise, but the B & O was not interested, and no progress was made.

Finally, by early 1871, opposition to the Union Railroad had abated and construction was resumed. An engineering feat was the construction of the Hoffman Street Tunnel, still used by passenger trains travelling north and south through Baltimore. Three hundred men labored from May 1, 1871 until July 25, 1873 in the tunnel's construction, laying nearly 9,000,000 bricks. The result was an underground passageway 3,405 feet long, costing in excess of $3,000,000. Completion of the Union Railroad created the first series of links connecting rail lines from the west, north and east to the port. Now that the Northern Central Railway could reach the Canton waterfront via the Union Railroad connection, the company felt it was necessary to provide such facilities as grain elevators and coal and cargo piers for volume traffic. In 1874 the Northern Central allocated $2,000,000 for construction of two cargo piers and a grain elevator on South Clinton Street in Canton.

An early view of Pennsylvania Railroad Canton terminal

Peale Museum

By 1875 the grain elevators at Locust Point and Canton were instrumental in bringing Midwest wheat into Baltimore for shipment to European markets. Between 1867 and 1880, the port's wheat exports rose in value from less than $1,000 to $43,500,000. At the same time two new coal piers were being built: Baker and Whitely's on South Clinton Street and the Philadelphia, Wilmington and Baltimore Railroad (later PRR) pier at the foot of East Avenue. These new installations and the one already in operation in Locust Point enabled Baltimore to become the leading coaling station for ocean-going ships on the East Coast.

In 1874, *Scribner's Magazine,* observing Baltimore's rapid development, declared that it had become "the Liverpool of America." Two years later the port ranked as the sixth largest in the world, its status attained largely by the movement of heavy commodities to and from the Midwest. While general cargo was never neglected, these heavy movements gave Baltimore the reputation of being primarily a "bulk" port which endured up to World War II.

The B & O began construction of its extension from Philadelphia to Baltimore in 1883. After many delays the work was completed on May 25, 1886. On July 11 of that year a Baltimore-Philadelphia freight service was started and on September 18 passenger service between the two cities began. As the B & O had no track through the city, two large ferries, the *John W. Garrett* and the *Canton,* transferred trains to and from Canton and Locust Point. The ferries remained in service until the Howard Street tunnel was completed in 1895. Most important, the Canton area of the port was now served by two important railroads, the Northern Central and the Baltimore and Ohio.

Baltimore had strong passenger connections with Bremen. During the Thirties and Forties, she attracted more Germans than any other port. The service was especially lucrative since a full return cargo of tobacco was always assured. Many of these vessels were Baltimore-built but flew the German flag. Usually of 1,000 to 1,500 tons gross register, they carried about a dozen cabin passengers and 150 to 500 in steerage. Under favorable conditions, the crossing would take about a month, but one passage in particularly bad weather took 103 days.

Conditions in the packet service were usually deplorable by the Fifties. The law allowed each passenger but 2 x 7 feet, and often 700 to 1000 immigrants were crowded on a deck of less than 200 feet. Naturally, loss of life was appalling under such circumstances. In 1853, for instance, out of 28 successive ships carrying 13,762 passengers 1,141 passengers died on the way over. And disasters were all too common—one of the most tragic being that of the seventeen-year-old Baltimore ship, *Powhatan*, which was driven aground on the New Jersey coast during a gale and broke up in full view of hundreds of spectators on shore who were unable to save any of the 200 German immigrants.

Conditions improved during the late 1800s as indicated by this article which appeared in *The Sun* on April 23, 1881:

> The North German Lloyd steamship *Strassburg* arrived last night with 1,680 immigrants—1,073 adults, 436 children and 171 infants, plus a general cargo. The state of health was very satisfactory, there being six deaths among the children and two births.

The sailing vessels carrying the immigrants to Baltimore berthed at County Wharf, on Thames Street between Broadway and Ann. County Wharf was also the scene of a colorful tradition. When a German brewmaster would sail for a vacation in the homeland, a major part of the German quarter would turn out to bid farewell. A beer wagon would be sent to the wharf and by the time the brewmaster and his family arrived in their coach, the party and folk singing were well under way.

Immigrants ready to debark at Locust Point, about 1910   *Peale Museum*

Spurred by the energy of its thousands of new immigrant citizens, Baltimore's industries grew enormously. One of the most modern steel plants in the United States was built at Sparrows Point during the years 1887 and 1891 by the Maryland Steel Co., a division of the Pennsylvania Steel Company, whose plant and headquarters were at Steelton, Pa. As the plant was dependent largely upon foreign ores from Cuba and Spain, two new piers were built, one 400, the other 600 feet long, with a water depth of 28 feet. The property consisted of 1,000 acres, and after the plant was completed the company built over 500 dwellings for officers and employees.

Those who designed and built the plant were the pioneers whose example has been so generally followed until now that it constitutes standard American practice. From an economic point of view, too, the officers of the company anticipated developments which were soon to come. They foresaw the opportunity to compete in the world's markets and it was done at a time when no one in steel dreamed that the day of export trade was approaching. The Maryland Steel Company shipped steel rails and billets to South Africa, Australia, India, England, Canada, Mexico, Venezuela and Argentina.

This move revived an earlier iron business that had depended on a domestic supply but which after the Civil War had slumped to near-extinction in the face of competition from newly built Ohio River mills, close to the sources of ore.

Maryland Steel Plant, Sparrows Point, 1890

Maryland Historical Society

THE TWENTIETH CENTURY—THE MODERN PORT: 1900–1950

BALTIMORE, THEN THE sixth largest city with 539,000 inhabitants, entered the twentieth century with flags flying. But a fire that started on Sunday morning, February 7, 1904 in the basement of a building that stood between Hopkins Place and Liberty Street on the south side of German (now Redwood) Street resulted in the greatest disaster ever to strike the 175-year-old city. Before the fire was brought under control on Monday afternoon it had burned out the downtown district of almost 140 acres, destroying some 1,500 buildings.

The wharves along Pratt Street as far as Jones Falls were swept by flames. Harold A. Williams, in his book, "Baltimore Afire" wrote, "Shortly after midnight (Sunday) the vessels on the north side of the basin were getting ready to move. When the flames began to lap at Pratt Street all the ships and smaller craft seemed to move at once toward the lower harbor. There was such an exodus of steamers, bay schooners, barges and tugs that collisions could be avoided only with difficulty. Some tugs from the lower harbor created additional confusion and jams by moving toward the Pratt Street docks to help with the rescue work." Total damage was estimated at between $125,000,000 and $150,000,000.

But rebuilding soon got underway, many streets were widened and other improvements made. As noted in "Baltimore Afire"—"The fire—first regarded as the greatest misfortune ever to strike Baltimore—really did more for the city than any other single act in its entire history. It is highly doubtful that Baltimore, on its own initiative, would ever have risen from its ancient thralldom of narrow streets, rotting wharves and antiquated buildings. It would have been difficult, if not impossible, to obtain the consent of the citizens to tearing out the very heart of Baltimore—no matter how splendid the plans for rebuilding might have been. But the obliging fire did it in one great swoop—making possible a new start for the twentieth century."

With a growing demand for new port facilities, the Canton Company decided to develop its property in lower Canton east of Lazaretto Point, into a modern, deepwater marine terminal. In 1906 the board of directors authorized the building of a railroad to enhance the development of the property and give the new marine terminal connections with the three major railroads entering Baltimore.

The Western Maryland Railway wanted an "outlet to tidewater" soon after the company was incorporated. But it was not until 1865 that it proposed building a line paralleling the Northern Central tracks from Relay House to Bolton Station in Baltimore. This would have given Western Maryland an outlet to tidewater at Canton but the proposal was rejected by the Northern Central.

On December 14, 1883 the Western Maryland Tidewater Railroad Company was incorporated. On March 24 the Maryland General Assembly amended the charter, authorizing the company "to construct, maintain and operate . . . elevators, wharves,

Baltimore from Federal Hill after Great Fire of 1904

piers, shops and other works necessary or proper . . . also purchase and own, hire or charter, steam or other vessels and use the same on the navigable waters of this state for the purpose of transporting passengers and freight to or from its railroad." But despite the charter, there were no immediate plans for constructing the tidewater outlet.

In the spring of 1902 the long-sought outlet finally became a reality. Within days after the Fuller Syndicate had purchased Baltimore City's interest in the Western Maryland—in May, 1902—surveys were made for the tidewater line from the road's main line at Walbrook Junction—on the outskirts of the city then—across Liberty, Franklin and Frederick roads, following Gwynns Falls to the Middle Branch of the Patapsco River at Winans Cove. Work began in November. To reach tidewater it was necessary to make cuts, some 40 feet deep and 1,000 long, and to span the Patapsco, where it was about a half-mile wide, with a draw-bridge. The terminal, near the site of Fort Covington, which played an important role in the defense of Baltimore during the War of 1812, consisted of about 25 acres with an 814 foot waterfront. About 100,000 cubic yards of dirt were removed to level the area; some 500,000 cubic yards of mud and sand were dredged in digging channels and anchorages.

The original facilities consisted of a 600-foot bulkhead, a freight pier, a coal pier and a transfer bridge for the interchange of cars between rail and barge. The freight pier and transit shed was 120 by 840 feet with two rail tracks alongside. The coal pier, 60 by 729 feet, had 40 coal chutes with a capacity of handling 1,000 tons per hour.

The Port Covington terminal was opened September 24, 1904. An article in *The Sun* the next day declared, "Without ostentation the new tidewater line of the Western Maryland Railroad was formally opened for traffic yesterday. A number of officials of the road visited the terminals of Port Covington to witness the modest beginning of what is the last link to the Atlantic of the Gould transcontinental system."

The terminal's business was sporadic and limited until the Cumberland extension, connecting the Western Maryland with the West Virginia Central and Pittsburgh, was opened. Then tonnage drawn from the East and Midwest poured through Port Covington. To handle the increased business, an open pier was added in 1912, and a grain elevator with an original capacity of 1,000,000 bushels was built.

Merchandise and coal pier, Western Maryland Railway, Port Covington, 1904

The opening of the Panama Canal in 1914 provided Baltimore with another advantage over the more northerly ports, enabling it to move for many years more west-bound tonnage through the new waterway than any of its Atlantic competitors.

The Bethlehem Steel Corporation acquired the Maryland Steel Company in 1916 and proceeded to expand the Sparrows Point installation for greater steel manufacturing and shipbuilding.

For many years one of the most important assets of the port was the Cottman crane pier in Lower Canton. In 1879, Clarence Cottman founded a company to stevedore and weigh cargo. It was incorporated on November 20, 1916 to operate and carry on the business of stevedoring ship brokerage and agency, public weight, storage, warehousing and forwarding.

Construction of Pier 1, Pratt Street, December 5, 1908   *Author's Collection*

In January, 1917 the Cottman Company leased a pier the Canton Company was constructing in Lower Canton. It was 88 feet wide, 1,253 feet long, had a depth of 35 feet on both sides and was served by four railroad tracks. Cottman installed a new bridge crane capable of discharging over 400 tons of bulk material an hour.

An increased demand for modern facilities for bunkering and loading coal for shipment to Europe took place in the early 1900's. The Pennsylvania Railroad purchased the antiquated Baker-Whitely coal pier in Canton and built a new facility. Completed in 1917, it was 910 feet long with a loading capacity of 900 tons per hour. The same year the B & O finished building its new coal pier in Curtis Bay, 700 feet long with a loading capacity of 800 tons per hour. On September 5, 1919, the Western

Maryland's coal pier at Port Covington was almost destroyed by fire. Two years later it was replaced with a modern structure, completed on April 1, 1921. With these facilities the port became the East Coast's leading coaling station.

Baltimore, with her many sundry industries and waterfront facilities, had a major role in supplying the needs of our armed forces during World War I. The Quartermaster Corps of the U.S. Army built a supply depot in Lower Canton 1,000 feet from the waterfront. The depot, called Colgate, consisted of four groups of warehouses totaling 750,000 square feet of floor space. There were 36 sections with concrete floors and wide platforms, each with rail sidings and truck loading facilities. The officer in command was Captain W. G. N. Rukert, whose career on the Baltimore waterfront was just beginning.

World War I did not strain the port to the extent it would be during World War II, but it did reveal inadequacies which Baltimoreans had been too busy to notice. The dominant railroads, already feeling the first thrust of automobile and truck competition, seemed reluctant to supply the necessary improvements. But the State of Maryland, recognizing the importance of modern facilities, in 1920 passed an enabling act providing up to $50,000,000 for major harbor improvements.

Had all the recommendations embodied in a 1922 survey of Baltimore harbor been carried out, Port Covington today would total nine piers, instead of three. And a giant cold storage warehouse would stand at the foot of Federal Hill.

The survey was drawn up by the Port Development Commission under the chairmanship of John E. Greiner. It had been created to administer the Port Development Act, which authorized the $50,000,000 bond issue.

Canton Company terminals, 1918

Author's Collection

The Port—Pride of Baltimore / 67

McComas Street terminals

Western Maryland Railway

Bancroft Hill, the harbor engineer, made two studies of the port for the commission. One listed actual facilities, the other outlined possible improvements. A companion piece to his four volume report was a survey by the New York firm of Clapp and Stuart for which the commission paid $10,000. Edwin J. Clapp handled the commercial phase of the 1922 report, while Francis Lee Stuart, a former chief engineer of the B & O, concentrated on facilities and physical improvements.

The Port Development Commission studied both reports, combined their best features, and in March, 1922, issued its own over-all development plan which included:

1—*Port Covington*—Construction of nine piers, each 1,200 feet long eight for general use, either individually or in groups, with the ninth exclusive for government vessels. Behind them 25 warehouses were planned, as were train yard and roads for motor traffic. Together the piers were to be able to handle 33 vessels at a time. The commission, in its enthusiasm, had a sketch drawn of the proposed terminal. It jammed the dock area with practically every type vessel from three-masted sailing vessels to four-funneled steamers.

2—Similiar piers and warehouses, plus a 2,500-foot marginal wharf, were planned for the reclaimed Patapsco on the southside of Locust Point along with switching yards to accommodate 4,900 railroad cars.

3—*Canton*—The commission suggested that from Point Breeze to the foot of Newkirk Avenue four solid fill piers each 1,000 feet long with two 1,200 foot piers projecting from the end of each. The piers were designed to hold 66 vessels and supported by warehouses and a rail yard with a 11,500 car capacity.

4—The property at Hughes Street and Key Highway would be used for a large cold storage warehouse.

5—The commission recommended unification of port control and operation, and urged Baltimore to create a free-trade zone.

Conceived in a boom period, most of the suggested improvements disappeared in the retrenchment that followed the Depression.

The commission did make possible the McComas Street Terminals at Port Covington for the Western Maryland Railway, but the proposed additional facilities along the shore to Fort McHenry were not built until 58 years later.

In 1929 the Port Development Commission built the McComas Street Terminal and leased it to the Western Maryland Railway under an extendable 30-year contract. Eight large ocean-going vessels could dock at the three new piers. The piers were supplemented by transit sheds containing 599,771 square feet of floor space and a rail holding yard for 3,000 cars. In a telegram to the mayor of Baltimore, Thomas A. Edison described the opening "as an important event in the era of modern transportation."

After the war new industries appeared on the Baltimore waterfront, capitalizing on the desirable tidewater location providing easy access to import raw materials and facilitating exportation of finished products. In 1921 the Pennsylvania Railroad began construction of a pier and grain elevator at the foot of Newkirk Street. Completed in 1923 at a cost of $6,000,000, with a capacity of over 4,000,000 bushels, it was the largest and most modern elevator on the Atlantic seaboard. That same year the Canton Company finished building Pier 8, an important part of its now extensive deepsea waterfront terminal. Despite the slowdown in the economy after World War I and the crash of 1929 and ensuing Depression, the port did not suffer as badly as other East Coast ports because three national industries selected sites in the Canton area for expansion programs.

The American Radiator & Standard Sanitary Corporation constructed a plant in 1924 for the manufacture of enameled cast iron bathtubs. In 1926 the Gold Dust Corporation (now Lever Brothers) opened a plant for the manufacture of soap products In the late 1920s, the increasing needs of the nation's telephone system spurred Western Electric to find another manufacturing site. After an extensive survey of East Coast port cities Baltimore was selected because of its excellent rail and water facilities. In 1929 Western Electric purchased the Riverview amusement park at Point Breeze. In less than a year after ground was broken, the plant produced its first reels of cable.

In the spring of 1931 the Canton Company added a new pier to its expanding deepwater marine terminal. Pier 11 was 1,643 feet long supported by a modern two-story fireproof transit shed. The facility was turned over to the Pennsylvania Railroad with a long term lease.

The United States Lines used this as the terminal for its subsidiary, the Baltimore Mail Steamship Company, a new passenger and freight service to Europe. The flow of cargo and passengers across the Atlantic was resumed after a lapse of fourteen years, when the Port of Baltimore was without regular liner service to Europe.

The *City of Baltimore,* flagship of the fleet, sailed from Pier 11 on her maiden voyage on July 2, 1931. She is said to have received one of the greatest salutes the city has ever given a ship on her first voyage. A large silver service was presented to her captain by Mayor Howard Jackson.

The Baltimore Mail Steamship Company continued to operate until the beginning of World War II when the U.S. Maritime Commission took over the fleet and converted the vessels into military transports.

On July 17, 1932, a fire destroyed a large portion of the Pennsylvania Railroad's marine terminal in Canton. Three piers, an office building, and a number of freight cars were damaged beyond repair. Because of the importance of this terminal, the railroad decided to replace the damaged wooden piers with a modern fireproof structure. The new pier was opened September 1, 1934. It was 930 feet long by 223 feet wide and had the necessary facilities for handling passengers and import and export freight. Its pier space was sufficient to accommodate four ocean-going vessels at one time. It cost more than $14,000,000.

Business continued to increase rapidly for Rukert Terminals Corporation following the Depression so further expansion was planned. The pier at Jackson's Wharf could not be lengthened for technical reasons. Lengthening would have interfered with the "Port Warden" line and safety requirements of the Corps of Engineers, so the company began a search for a new site in the Canton area.

In 1937 Rukert Terminals entered into a 99-year lease with the Pennsylvania Railroad for its Pier 5 facility at 2100 South Clinton Street, Canton. The property included six acres of open land and a 400-foot pier. The first step in development of this property was building a warehouse 350 by 125 feet to handle import potash.

During the next decade 39 overseas steamship lines sailed regularly to the port, along with thirteen coastal and nine intercoastal services. Baltimore had gained the reputation as the best U.S. port for the finest record for tons per hour and the lowest stevedoring costs—thanks to a stable International Longshoreman Union, then headed by two capable men—Jefferson Davis and August Idzik.

At the outbreak of World War II coastwise and intercoastal services were suspended as the U.S. Maritime Commission took over the majority of the vessels and converted them into military transports.

In the spring of 1941, the schooner *Harriet C. Whitehead* loaded a cargo of bulk Russian potash (a fertilizer ingredient) in Baltimore, the potash being consigned to an Eastern Shore fertilizer plant. This was the beginning of the end of sailing vessels transporting cargo on the Bay—victims to the increased use of trucks and an expanding highway system. For over 200 years beautiful schooners, bugeyes and rams had been carrying raw materials to plants on the Eastern Shore of Maryland and Virginia and returning with shore produce and lumber from the sawmills on the Western Shore of Virginia.

During the war, with a great demand for sailing craft to carry cargoes between Florida and the West Indies, many of the schooners sailed out of the Chesapeake Bay forever. With the increased need for speed many of the remaining craft were converted to powerboats.

In 1942 the Transportation Corps of the U.S. Army took over Canton Company's Pier 11-Pier 10 complex as a major supply base for the European Theatre. It became the most efficient and productive base on the eastern seaboard.

During the next five years Baltimore's port and industries operated at peak efficiency, establishing new world records for performance. The Bethlehem-Fairfield shipyards produced more vessels—384 new Liberty ships alone—than any other yard in the nation. It is worth noting that its all-out wartime efforts did not exhaust the ingenuity of Baltimore's shipbuilders. By 1950, when many of the war-built ships were becoming uneconomical to operate, yet too new and valuable to scrap, the Maryland Shipbuilding and Drydock Company devised the process of "jumbo-izing" many of these vessels by inserting longer midbodies, increasing carrying capacity by as much as 50 percent. This has since revolutionized ship renovation around the world.

The strain of war on available facilities pointed up a number of weaknesses. The dominant railroads, feeling the full impact of highway competition, were not willing to repair and modernize their antiquated piers. The excitement of victory had hardly subsided when business leaders began talking about the best way to insure the port's future growth.

On May 26, 1949 the Baltimore Association of Commerce authorized the firm of Knappen Tippetts Abbett Engineering Company of New York to survey the Port of Baltimore to appraise what existed and to ascertain what might be the best approach to future development.

The two-volume survey was presented to the Baltimore Association of Commerce on December 31, 1949 with the recommendation that the progressive expansion of the port should be on the basis of a Master Plan of Development arranged in three stages:

Stage I would embrace the rehabilitation and improvement of existing facilities, particularly for the accommodation of trucks, to the immediate benefit of the volume of general cargo now coming into the port, at an estimated cost of $18,600,000.

Stage II improvements and additions, at an estimated cost of $30,400,000, would supplement existing facilities. Upon completion, the port would be capable of handling the additional 2,500,000 tons of general cargo annually which the survey estimated could be attracted in the near future.

Stage III improvements, at a total estimated cost of $79,740,000, would develop the port progressively to meet the demands of increasing future commerce.

The study further recommended that private financing of the improvements should be encouraged. Only when this fails the Port District Commission should undertake financial aid to private interests to further the Master Plan of Port Development. If private capital or private financing, with the assistance of public funds should not prove successful in furthering the program of essential improvements, then the Port District Commission should provide directly the facilities and services required in the interests of the general public and of industry.

Despite the deterioration of the general cargo piers new facilities were constructed and others upgraded to handle bulk materials.

The National Gypsum Company, one of the nation's largest manufacturers of building materials, opened a plant in Canton in the fall of 1947. It represented an investment of about $8,000,000. In addition to the plant constructed by National Gypsum, it involved a $1,500,000 investment by the City of Baltimore in a pier for unloading bulk gypsum rock from Nova Scotia.

Rukert Terminals Corporation purchased 11 acres at Lazaretto Point in Canton from the Western Maryland Railway. Improvements to the property included the building of two marginal piers and 275,000 feet of modern warehouse space. For the next fifteen years this facility was used for the bagging of bulk sulphate of ammonia for export.

On June 30, 1950, the Canton Company gained control of the Cottman Company and installed a third bridge crane. The next year the B & O opened a new ore pier it had constructed in Curtis Bay. The pier was 650 feet long and equipped with two bridge cranes.

Author's Note: The second half of the 20th century is dealt with in the chapter headed "Maryland Port Administration," starting on page 105.

Lazaretto Point Terminal, 1967

Author's Collection

THE CHANNEL DEEPENS AND THE C & D CANAL

FROM ALMOST ITS beginning the port has been concerned about its channel. As early as April 23, 1735 the Maryland General Assembly dealt with it and related matters. On that date it passed an act to prevent the injuring of harbors within the Province. Scharf reports that "By this act masters of vessels and others were prohibited, under the penalty of 50 pounds currency, from casting ballast into the bay above Cedar Point, nor into any river, creek or harbor below high-water mark, nor to unload ballast but between the rising and the setting of the sun." For many years much money and energy was expended to deepen the harbor basin, in places only two feet deep. In the early years much of the port activities were centered in the Fells Point area where the average depth was 16 feet. A practical scheme, said to be the first attempt to deepen any American harbor, began in 1783. This involved an iron scoop drag, drawn by oxen, horses and sometimes manpower. Interest in dredging the harbor remained strong following this cumbersome attempt and in 1826 Watchman and Bratt of Federal Hill were awarded the contract to construct a floating steam-powered dredge after producing a model and selling the scheme to the city. The twelve-horsepower steam engine and dredge were delivered on April 1, 1827 at a cost of $19,000 (today this would not buy a scow used to haul dredge spoil).

Outer harbor improvements were the responsibility of the Federal government. As early as 1826 the Secretary of the Navy submitted a report on a survey of the harbor to Congress. The depth of the main channel at mean low water measured 17 feet. The secretary noted "the water can be readily, and at inconsiderable expense, deepened to 20 feet, by means of the admirable mud-excavators now in operation in the harbor." In 1830 army engineers surveyed the harbor, and in 1836 $20,000 was appropriated for deepening the entrance channels. The law stipulated no specific dimensions. Congress gave the money to the Board of Port Wardens which used it to hire the city's dredging apparatus. By 1838 an additional $35,000 in Federal money had been spent on dredging the Patapsco. The army engineers requested that Congress appropriate $25,000 annually for harbor maintenance. But the river and harbor improvements encountered vociferous political and constitutional criticism after 1838. The harbor received no more Federal funds until 1852.

It was in that year that efforts to develop an adequate channel really began when Captain Henry Brewerton arrived in Baltimore. He became the Baltimore District Engineer in 1852 and his first task was to examine various dredging machines. He envisioned that three would be necessary to excavate the Patapsco to a depth of 22 feet. He finally settled on a single bucket dredge that could excavate about 100 cubic yards of mud per hour.

Captain Henry Brewerton   *National Archives*

By November, 1853 it and a single dipper dredge the city had ordered were working in the Patapsco River in two areas. The upper branch started at Fort McHenry and extended six miles to a point one-and-a-half miles below Fort Carroll. The average natural depth ranged from 19 to 21 feet. The lower division ran nine miles from the point one-and-a-half miles below Fort Carroll to four miles beyond North Point. The average depth was only 16 to 18 feet.

Brewerton concentrated his efforts on the lower branch. His goal was to form a channel 150 feet wide and 22 feet deep. In July, 1854, the city added a third dredge. In 1857 the Federal Government contributed two more dredges and a tug boat. By the end of 1858 the channel could support vessels drawing about 20 feet of water. A survey made a year later showed that six miles of the channel had been dredged to an average depth of $23\frac{1}{2}$ feet. Brewerton urged that the channel be completed as soon

Brigadier Major William P. Craighill

as possible so that it could be used by the largest class of vessels wanting to use the port. He wanted $100,000 for the channel for the next fiscal year. No new money was forthcoming and operations were suspended.

The Board of Commissioners of Baltimore named the channel Brewerton, in honor of their district engineer, whose tireless energy had made the excavation a success. When work resumed in 1866 the first project was to measure the Brewerton Channel as the lower portion heading straight into the Chesapeake Bay had shoaled considerably. Major William P. Craighill, who became the District Engineer in November, 1865 proposed that a new cut be constructed to alter the direction of the channel. Instead of going straight into the Bay, it would run due south for about three miles and then turn in a southeasterly direction. This course would correspond to the current of the Patapsco and Susquehanna Rivers and shorten the distance to

Baltimore by about three-and-one-half miles.

While Craighill served as assistant to the Chief of Engineers in Washington from October 19, 1866 until March 31, 1870, Major General John G. Parke and Colonel John H. Simpson supervised the digging of the new cut. The goal was a channel 200 feet wide and 22 feet deep. It was Simpson who designated this the Craighill Channel, and in October, 1869 it was opened to vessels drawing less than 21 feet.

By 1870 the Baltimore Harbor compared favorably with all other Atlantic ports as 735 foreign vessels entered the harbor compared to 650 in 1869. In the first half of 1871 the total reached 508 ships. The port of Baltimore was prospering. About this time the dumping of dredged material had become a hotly debated issue. The controversy has persisted to the present day.

Baltimore's leaders desired that the port continue to grow. The Baltimore City Council, the Board of Trade and the Corn and Flour Exchange all urged Craighill to push for a deeper approach channel. The Corn and Flour Exchange went so far as to ask the city to appropriate massive funds for the improvement of the harbor to a depth of 24 feet without waiting for Congress to act. *The Sun* joined those who sought money to dredge the Patapsco River leading to the inner port. To the paper, a Federal appropriation of at least $300,000 would be reasonable. "Our representatives in Congress should direct their earnest and united efforts," the paper exhorted, "to secure, at the earliest possible day, such an appropriation."

The campaign for a large infusion of funds for harbor improvement paid off handsomely in 1872. That year the city organized a Board of Improvement and provided it with $200,000 for immediate expenditure on the harbor. Congress appropriated $100,000. Craighill supervised the concurrent Federal and city operations.

During the spring of 1872 he revised the entire project. Now it would be possible to widen and deepen the harbor approaches on a massive scale. The goal expanded to a channel 24 feet deep throughout. In addition, the width would be enlarged to 250 feet from Fort McHenry through the Brewerton Channel and to 400 feet through the hard lumps of the lower Craighill Channel. The widening of the Brewerton Channel was completed by the end of 1872.

Because of successful cooperative effort, Craighill could report by the end of 1874 that he had completed the entire channel to its projected depth and width. At the turn from the Brewerton to the Craighill Channel, an angle of 90 degrees, the width was 1,000 feet to facilitate easy turns by larger vessels. No dramatic changes were made in the Patapsco channels between 1874 and 1881.

Working behind the scenes, Craighill wrote John Garrett, B & O president, in 1880 suggesting a plan to quickly get money from Congress for the expansion of the harbor. He told Garrett that the cost of dredging the channel to a 27-foot depth would be $1,500,000.

Craighill's efforts were rewarded in 1881 when Congress approved a project to deepen the channel to that depth. Because of an insufficient number of large dredges, excavation on the new project started slowly. But a substantial dredging force and a $450,000 appropriation in 1882 expedited the work. The achievement of the 27-foot depth took until the end of 1884.

Upon completion of the dredging Craighill ordered a survey of the channel to verify progress. It showed considerable shoaling along the sides of the Craighill and Brewerton channels caused by large vessels striking the banks and sending masses of material into the dredged harbor approaches. The implication was obvious, the channel had to be wider, but operations were suspended because of insufficient funds during the fiscal year ending June 30, 1886.

Meanwhile Craighill continued to campaign privately for more funds. Sometimes his desire for Baltimore to become the country's principal commercial center superseded his duties as engineer. He was particularly anxious that the port's reputation not be damaged by bad publicity. Fortunately he had cordial relations with members of Congress. He corresponded frequently with Maryland Senator Arthur Pue Gorman on the need for more money. "I was very anxious indeed," Senator Gorman assured Craighill in 1887, "to have you begin at an early day the widening of the channel and complete that work, so that it will remain always as a monument to your skill as an engineer." According to the Senator, no officer in the Corps carried as much weight with the Senate Committee on Commerce as did the Baltimore District engineer.

When Gorman asked Craighill for a confidential letter outlining the need for a large appropriation, Craighill responded by urging a grant of not less than $600,000. He received half that amount. Nevertheless, Congress, in its Rivers and Harbors Act of 1888, did officially authorize a main channel width of 600 feet. By December, 1892 and almost a $1,000,000 later, Baltimore had a channel of 27 feet deep and 600 feet wide.

One of the major projects of the 1890's was the dredging of Curtis Bay, a tributary of the Patapsco River, to connect it with the main channel. Congress approved the Curtis Bay project in 1892 providing for a channel 150 wide and 25 feet deep, which was completed in 1894. By 1898 the amount of annual commerce passing through the port had increased $107,687,375 in value since the beginning of major improvements in 1852.

Craighill, who arrived in Baltimore as a major, left after 30 years in 1895 to become the Chief of Engineers in Washington as a brigadier general. *The Sun* wished him well in his new position and thanked him for "securing a splendid deep-water channel for the expanding commerce of this port." The Baltimore *American* editorialized: "To the man who brought the world's commerce into the port of Baltimore and thereby did much to revive the pristine glory of the days of the Clipper ships, under the new conditions of ocean liners, this city will always be indebted."

Craighill was obviously emotionally attached to Baltimore and he wanted to see his city gain prominence among its commercial rivals. He believed that not only should the harbor be dredged deeper, but the city should push for a modern sea-level canal to connect the Chesapeake and Delaware Bays. The following account will prove he was a man of intelligence and foresight.

On March 3, 1905 Congress authorized dredging the approach channels to the port to a depth of 35 feet. This was completed in 1915 at a cost of almost $4,000,000.

Following World War II Congress did revise the Baltimore Harbor project providing for a channel depth of 39 feet throughout. In 1946 and 1947 dredging by contract created a connecting channel 27 feet deep and 400 feet wide between Baltimore and the Chesapeake and Delaware Canal. New excavations and maintenance dredging continued simultaneously until 1954 when the 39 foot depth was achieved at a cost of about $15,000,000.

The first priority for the newly-created Maryland Port Authority in 1956 was a deeper and wider channel to accommodate the increasing size of ocean-going vessels. It spearheaded the port community campaign for Federal approvals and appropriations for the millions of dollars needed to accomplish the necessary dredging. It organized local presentations before Congress, assisted the Corps of Engineers in planning, and represented the Port in compliance with local obligations.

The project consisted of deepening and widening the main Baltimore Channel from the Virginia Capes as well as the branch channels within Baltimore Harbor. The previous depth had been 39 feet and the width generally 600 feet. The new width would be 800 feet although it is wider (1,000 feet) in the lower Bay and at the Capes. The project also included deepening and widening the $5\frac{1}{2}$-mile long connecting channel between Baltimore Harbor and the Chesapeake & Delaware Canal access channel.

Congress authorized the project in 1958 and work started in September, 1961. The authorizing legislation contained the usual "local cooperation" clause requiring that local interests provide necessary spoil disposal areas, and accomplish, without expense to the United States, any necessary alterations in sewers, water supply, drainage and other utilities.

A heavy dredge deepens the channel, about 1966

A. Aubrey Bodine

For the channel outside of the harbor, the Corps of Engineers was able to use overboard disposal. However, considerable difficulty was encountered in providing spoil disposal areas within the confines of the harbor. Bottom material typically is a fine-grained silt not suitable for fill material. Consequently land owners are generally unwilling to make their properties available for use as spoil disposal sites. Nevertheless, the Corps of Engineers insisted that they would not use any method more costly than hydraulic pipe line dredging which requires spoil disposal close to the location of the dredging. This precluded use of the deepwater spoil disposal area at Kent Island. To have the work proceed it was necessary for the Port Authority to find spoil disposal areas within the harbor area. The problem was solved in two ways:

1—The B & O and the Kennecott Refining Corporation, owners of adjacent tracts of waterfront land in the Marley Neck area, agreed to the construction of a diked spoil disposal area in front of their properties. This accommodated a substantial quantity of spoil from the lower reaches of the harbor channel.

2—Spoil from the remainder of the harbor channels was widely distributed into shallow areas in the vicinity of its point of generation. This technique, known as "spoil dispersal," was developed by the Corps of Engineers and the Authority's Engineering Department and used after the Authority had secured the cooperation of the majority of the riparian land owners adjacent to the disposal areas.

The project was finished in December, 1965 at a cost of $30,000,000, and only because of the outstanding cooperation of private business interests.

Twelve years of delay in developing a 50-foot channel has resulted in not only escalating costs but a flood of information and misinformation regarding its nature and need.

Following is a chronology of the efforts to deepen the channels from 42 to 50 feet wide and use Hart and Miller islands as a dredge disposal site. Clarence Long, Maryland's second district representative in Congress, has been a persistent foe of using that site because of ecological, economic and industrial reasons.

May 2, 1969—General Assembly approved Senate Bill No. 623. The bill provides $13,000,000 for the "design and construction of one or more diked disposal areas" to receive dredging from Baltimore Harbor.

Dec. 21, 1970—Green/Trident Report. Four volumes evaluating 70 potential disposal areas for dredgings. Recommended Hart/Miller site at estimated cost of $11,500,000.

Dec. 31, 1970—The River and Harbor Act authorized a Federal project to deepen the channels from 42 to 50 feet.

July 22, 1971—Representative Long voices concern about the ecological, economic and industrial effects of dumping at Hart/Miller Islands.

Feb. 14, 1972—Department of General Services estimates costs of $23,600,000 (including design and channels).

Feb. 19, 1974—Public Notice No. 022 Langenfelder and Son. Permit application to Corps of Engineers to construct stone bulkhead around Hart/Miller Islands.

Nov. 5, 1975—Board of Public Works final approval of Hart/Miller Island project.

June 20, 1977—Filing of Civil Action File No. HM-77-973, in U.S. District Court on behalf of Long's opposition group to Hart/Miller Island containment facility.

Jan. 11, 1978—State of Maryland purchased Hart/Miller Island from C. J. Langenfelder & Co.

Oct. 20, 1978—Judge Herbert L. Murray, U.S. District Court, rendered decision re Civil Action File No. HM-77-973. Court held that in issuing the permit, under 33 U.S.C. 403, the Corps of Engineers exceeded its authority.

Dec. 23, 1980—Judge Herbert L. Murray rejects suit filed by Long's opposition group.

Jan. 20, 1981—General Assembly authorized additional $23,000,000 to dike Hart/Miller Island.

July 14, 1981—Great Lakes Dredge and Dock Co. awarded a $32,000,000 contract to dike Hart/Miller Island.

Sept. 11, 1981—U.S. Senate appropriations subcommittee rejected any new water projects spending in fiscal year beginning October 1.

Sept. 15, 1981—Construction started of dike around Hart/Miller Island.

On January 25, 1982 President Reagan announced approval for the U.S. Corps of Engineers to begin dredging in the fall to deepen the channels from Cape Henry to Baltimore from 42 feet to 50 feet.

Dredging Baltimore shipping channels to 50 feet will double the size of vessels able to call here, especially helping the ore, grain and emerging coal trade.

Other benefits of the port dredging project could be increased construction employment in the Baltimore area while the dredging is done over four years and a permanent increase in stevedoring jobs and tonnage of shipping business.

Before the port dredging project can begin, many crucial issues must be resolved.

The major issue of how to finance the $332,500,000 dredging project still is unresolved. Traditionally, the Federal government has paid for all dredging projects and maintenance involving major navigational channels. But under President Reagan's administration's austere budget policies, the government now wants to recover some, if not all, of those funds.

President Reagan announced approval of a plan in which the Maryland state government would pay for 75 percent of the dredging cost, and the Federal government would help finance 25 percent with loans, not grants. Reagan's approval only covers the project's first year costs of $7,500,000 but officials hope that once the massive project begins, later funding approvals will be automatic.

The above plan would force the state to finance the project in one of three ways:

1—The Federal Government would lend the money to the state and the state would impose user fees to reimburse the government. All vessels using the channel would pay an undetermined per ton charge.

2—The state would finance the project by floating a bond issue and then pay the bonds off with funds collected through user fees.

3—The state would try to attract private investors to pay for the project and pay them back with user fees.

The 1971 Congress had approved a deeper channel for Baltimore but legal entanglements prevented Federal appropriation to begin the project.

With the assistance of Representative Long, the environmentalists and other opponents of the dredging plan's spoil-storage proposal managed to delay the project for 10 years. And by the time they had retired from the fight a new administration, with radically different ideas about financing major public-works projects, was determining policy.

It is impossible to ascertain what the port has lost during the last 10 years due to the opposition of the environmentalists' group. We do know that the cost of diking Hart/Miller Island has risen from $13,000,000 to a estimated $60,000,000 and the cost of dredging the 50-foot channel has doubled.

Millions of dollars from the state's economy was lost during this period due to the inability of loading grain vessels to capacity. Hundreds of vessels were loaded to 42 feet ($2/3$ of capacity) and then sailed to Norfolk to be topped off. One can only guess what impact this has had on Bethelem Steel's Sparrows Point plant which is importing ore in smaller vessels instead of super-bulk carriers.

THE C&D CANAL

Baltimore is regarded as the only port on the eastern seaboard possessing two exits to the sea. Its principal route, naturally, is via Chesapeake Bay to the Virginia Capes, 150 nautical miles. The other route is through the Chesapeake and Delaware Canal to the Delaware Capes, about 125 nautical miles.

As a trade route, the Chesapeake Bay probably always will be the most important avenue for sea traffic, but the canal saves distance and time on passages to northern American and European ports. For example, a ship that uses the Chesapeake and Delaware Canal rather than the southern route can save 286 miles on a passage from Baltimore to Philadelphia. By way of the Virginia Capes the distance is 380 nautical miles; via the canal, 94 nautical miles.

The advantages of a canal between the Delaware River and Chesapeake Bay were realized as early as 1679. At that time, there was a cart road between the Bohemia River and Appoquinimink Creek for the transportation of goods between the Delaware River and Chesapeake Bay. However, it was not until 1764, and again in 1769, that surveys were made to determine the feasibility of joining Chesapeake Bay and the Delaware River.

In 1799 an act was passed by the Maryland Legislature incorporating the Chesapeake and Delaware Company. In 1804, after a further survey, the route proposed would connect the Elk River, Maryland with Christiana Creek in Delaware. But in 1806 after most of the feeder canal from Big Elk Creek had been dug, operations were abandoned in favor of a new route. This was to connect Broad Creek (off the Elk River) with St. Georges Creek in Delaware, practically the route of the present canal.

Work got under way, mostly with picks, shovels, and horsepower, in 1824. Progress was slow and the project costly. Financing was made possible through lotteries and grants from Maryland, Delaware, Pennsylvania and the Federal government. The waterway was officially opened on October 17, 1829. Shortly after its opening a passenger line of horse-drawn barges called the "Peoples Line" operated through the canal.

The eastern terminus was Delaware City, laid out in 1826. A canal level of 7.6 feet above mean low water in the Delaware River was maintained by a tide lock. Another lock in the vicinity of St. Georges, Delaware, raised the canal level an additional 10 feet. The next locks were at Chesapeake City, the western terminus.

There two locks permitted a descent of 15 feet to the level of Back Creek, an arm of the Elk River. The canal had a depth of 10 feet and a bottom width of 36 feet. The locks were 96 feet long, 22 feet wide with a depth of 8 feet of water over the sills.

As more and larger ships used it, extensive improvements were made, including enlarging the locks. For years towage for sailing ships and barges was by mules that walked the towpath paralleling the waterway. Later, shallow draft tugs were used.

The need for a deeper canal to permit the passage of larger vessels became apparent toward the latter part of the nineteenth century. Then the needs of World War I gave impetus to the transformation of the canal, and it was taken over by the Federal Government in 1919.

In 1921 work began to convert the old lock canal into a sea level, toll-free waterway, 12 feet deep at mean low water, with a bottom width of 90 feet. In May, 1927 it was completed to those dimensions. It was crossed by five vertical lift bridges providing horizontal clearances of 165 feet to 230 feet and a vertical clearance, when open, of 135 feet above mean low tide.

Early C & D Canal lock   *Army Corps of Engineers*

The Penn approaching Bucks Bridge before the canal was widened   *Collection of Robert H. Burgess*

Soon after those changes had been made, the need for a wider and deeper canal became evident because of the rapid increase in traffic, from 750,000 tons to about 2,000,000 tons in the Thirties. In 1935 enlargement of the canal to a depth of 27 feet and width of 250 feet was authorized. In December, 1939 the canal was opened to ships drawing 25 feet of water.

The rapid increase in traffic led to congressional authorization for a canal capable of handling ocean-going vessels and large barges. The result was a waterway 27 feet deep at mean low water and 250 feet wide in the easterly 18 miles and 400 feet wide for 22 miles to normal deep water in Chesapeake Bay. The course was also improved, but the sharp bends, narrow channel, and extremely narrow bridge clearances made the waterway a difficult one for navigation by large vessels. Two of the original bridges were destroyed by colliding ships. They were replaced by high-level bridges.

With the increase of traffic, tonnage grew from 2,000,000 tons to 9,000,000 tons annually. This was considered to be the economic limit of the canal. However, as new and larger ships were built, the demands on the canal increased, so Congress directed a new study and further improvement was authorized in 1954. The channel was realigned, deepened and widened and three new high-level bridges were built.

Today the fourteen-mile waterway is 35 feet deep at mean low tide, 450 feet wide at the bottom and extends 55 miles from natural deep water in Chesapeake Bay to the Delaware River.

In 1981 the tonnage was 15,950,000 tons, and there were 14,129 passages which included ships, tugs, barges and pleasure craft.

Passing under one of the canal's high-level bridges *Army Corps of Engineers*

BAY PILOTS AND CUSTOM HOUSES

EARLY BAY PILOTS in the late 1700's and early 1800's had to collect their own fees and supply their own boats, manned by at least two licensed partners and one apprentice. Sometimes there were as many as ten small pilot boats cruising outside the Capes awaiting vessels bound for Baltimore. When a sail was sighted on the horizon all would race to reach the inbound vessel. The winning boat would throw a line to the ship and the pilot would be put aboard to bring the ship up the Bay.

Life aboard the early pilot boats was hazardous, particularly in the days of sail, in the winter with gales and ice to fight. The pilot of the *Sterling* reported upon reaching Baltimore from the Capes that the pilot boat *Tally Ho* was out to sea on January 1, 1837 and encountered a heavy gale from the northwest while the weather was extremely cold. The boat was so loaded with ice on the forward part of the deck that it was bringing her down by the head and he was afraid they would have to run into the Gulf stream. Ten days later it was reported: "The pilot boat *Tally Ho* arrived at Norfolk all safe, having been driven off into the Gulf stream and been out to sea eight days." In the summer there were hurricanes. A report such as this was not uncommon, "The brig *Mary* and schooner *Amethyst* went to sea taking their pilots with them, the gale so severe that no boat could take them off." That meant the pilot was forced to stay aboard until the first port of call, returning to Baltimore by the next incoming vessel. According to one story, a pilot was on a vessel for 72 days before returning home.

Shortly before the formation of the Association of Maryland Pilots there were eight Baltimore pilot boats: *Comet, Selim, Liberty, Henry Clay, Baltimore, Tally Ho, Pocahontas,* and *Constitution*. All were main topmast schooners, and the hulls, with their clean sharp lines, resembled the Baltimore Clipper.

Each had six pilots in partnership. Earnings then were divided "in the boat" according to the partnership agreement. When a boat became worn out or too slow the group replaced her.

The Association of Maryland Pilots was organized in 1852 with offices at 83 Thames Street in Fells Point. At one time the initiation fee was $1,000 for which a pilot received an undivided non-transferable share in the property of the association. Membership was attained after a four-year apprenticeship and passing a stiff examination. Once a member, each man took his turn piloting a vessel to the Capes where he was picked up by the pilot boat and waited his turn to bring up an inbound vessel. All fees were collected by the association and once a month, after paying all expenses, including the cost of manning, victuals and maintaining the pilot boats, the remainder was divided among the pilots.

In addition to the regular pilotage fees, some incidental earnings were also

Maryland Pilot Boat "Commerce," 1836

Maryland Historical Society

divided. There were fines for pilots who refused their turn and for vessels which illegally traveled the Bay without taking a pilot or paying tonnage. Every year, at least up to 1860, the pilots put out new buoys or replaced damaged ones and were paid for these services. They also profited from the sale of old rope and sails. But the largest of all the incidental earnings was the salvage of property. For example, in May, 1858, Charles Nuthall paid the pilot $5 for a canoe evidently found adrift; in February, 1860 pilots were paid $150 for recovering the anchor and $75 for the hawser of the ship *Star*. Each of these laconic bookkeeper's entries could doubtless tell a story were the facts fully known. A somewhat fuller account was given for the collection of $750 from the schooner *Neptune's Bride:*

"30 November 1858. Disaster—Schr. *Neptune's Bride* at this port from New York, was fallen in with on Saturday last, off Cape Henry by pilot boat *Coquette*, who on boarding her found 4½ feet water in hold. She was supplied with six pilots who pumped her out and threw the deck load overboard. She reached this port yesterday."

In 1880 the Association built the steamer *Pilot*, said to be the first steam pilot boat in the United States. But even with boilers and engines the pilots retained the fore and main masts. With occasional refurbishing the *Pilot* stayed on duty until December, 1917.

Even with powerful engines, radio, and modern instruments, the work of the pilots today is not without danger. In 1917 the *Pilot* was run down and sunk by a Norfolk-bound steamer and in 1938 the *William D. Sanner* was rammed by the British ship *Levernbank*. Twenty-six men were on board, sixteen pilots and ten hands. Somehow all managed to squeeze into the small boats and were picked up by a Virginia pilot boat.

One of the most unusual requests made of a pilot occurred just before the United States entered into World War I.

On July 9, 1916 pilot Owen Coleman boarded the German submarine *Deutschland* at Cape Henry to bring her to Baltimore. The *Deutschland* had left Germany on June 13, 1916 with a cargo of dyestuff and other sophisticated products. Before beginning its return voyage August 1, Coleman was asked to accompany the submarine to Germany, so when it returned on its second trip it would not have to stop at the Capes for a pilot. The motive behind this was not known, but it was apparently to prevent the Allies from capturing or sinking the submarine.

If patrol boats would sink the submarine with an American aboard, England and the other Allies would find themselves involved in acute complications with the United States. There is little doubt that something along this line was actuating the move of the people behind the *Deutschland's* venture.

But the request was too transparent and Coleman refused to go. He pointed out that on her return the *Deutschland*, according to the pilot's regulations, would be compelled to take the "first man out," the pilot next on the waiting list on the pilot boat.

Today the Association of Maryland Pilots is a highly sophisticated organization. Applicants to become bay pilots must have a degree in Marine Transportation or Nautical Science. If accepted they must serve two years as trainees and four years as junior pilots before obtaining their licenses.

For almost one hundred and thirty years members of the Association of Maryland Pilots have served ships carrying the commerce that is the life-blood of the port of Baltimore. They have seen the Chesapeake Bay change from an unmarked, uncharted course, filled with dangers of shoals, fog, ice and sudden gales to one with the most modern aids for safe navigation.

Pilot boat, 1880

Maryland Historical Society

THE GERMAN U BOAT "DEUTSCHLAND" LARGEST IN THE WORLD AND HER COMMANDER-CAPTAIN KOENIG. ARRIVING BALTIMORE HARBOR-JULY 10TH 1916.

German U-Boat Deutschland, 1916

Author's Collection

Pilot Boat "Maryland," 1980

Painting by Brian Hope

CUSTOM HOUSES

Prior to the Revolutionary War Baltimore had a small office for the collection of revenue, but the custom house proper of those days was at Annapolis, a more important town. Among the archives of the Baltimore custom house the earliest book of records is dated 1769 and relates to the storage of flour. The next is for the year 1780, recording the entrance and clearance of vessels for the port. Some 250 vessels of all kinds, engaged in the foreign and coastwise trade, had been entered and cleared. The aggregate tonnage was only 13,000 tons, and the exports consisted almost entirely of tobacco and flour.

After the war and the adoption of the Federal Constitution the commerce of the port increased so much that it was necessary to establish a regular custom house for the collection of revenues. An act of Congress in 1786, created the Office of Collector of Customs, and prescribed the duties of the incumbent. Prior to the Revolution duties were collected by a naval officer, an official appointed by the Crown, who travelled by warship to the various ports of the province on stated occasions and gathered the revenues.

The first collector of customs after the Revolution was General Otho H. Williams, who was appointed by President Washington. The custom house in those days was in a small building on the northeast corner of Gay and Lombard Streets. In 1815 the Merchants and Exchange building was built at Gay and Water Streets. Designed by Benjamin H. Latrobe it was regarded as one of the seven wonders of the Jacksonian period. Latrobe, with Maximillian Godefroy, who also worked on the heroic Graeco-Roman design, put up what was the first commercial building of any size in America. It was also, after the Capitol and the White House, the nation's first extravagant building—and a more original one, at that, than either Washington structure.

This beautiful structure was built in the shape of an "H". The Government rented the first floor of the Gay Street wing for a custom house. Other sections were used by the Exchange Hotel and the Merchants Bank.

Old Custom House

Baltimore Sunpapers

Present Custom House

In 1851 the U. S. Government leased the rotunda for the post office where it remained for many years. Five years later the Government bought the entire building for $267,000.

According to reports, the bodies of President Abraham Lincoln, Henry Clay, Colonel Samuel Ringgold, who was killed in the Battle of Palo Alto during the war with Mexico, and Colonel William H. Watson and Captain Samuel Chase Ridgely, Marylanders who were slain in the battle of Monterey, lay in state in the rotunda. During the Civil War troops slept there while a cannon guarded the door.

Beaten to pieces by a variety of adaptive uses, it was razed by government order in 1901. Shortly after bids for the new custom house were opened in Washington in January 1902, Secretary of the Treasury Gage announced that Maryland granite would be used for the building and it would be constructed by a Baltimore firm, Henry Smith & Sons.

Ground was broken on March 6, 1902 by Collector William F. Stone. On June 13, 1903 the Grand Lodge of Masons of Maryland laid the cornerstone. It weighed more than eleven tons and was one of the largest at that time in the United States.

The beautiful new custom house with marble walls was opened on December 2, 1907. Built at a cost of nearly $2,000,000 it was six stories high, 250 feet long and 150 feet wide, and was described as the finest building outside of Washington. Designed by Hornblower and Marshall, of Washington, it is not only a particularly refined and subtly restrained design, but a fine example of a blending of art and architecture that flourished briefly in America around the turn of the century. The Call Room ceiling by Francis Davis Millet (1846–1912) is generally acknowledged to be the masterpiece of that important American artist. Millet's decorative design for the Call Room represents not only an aesthetic success of major significance in the history of American mural painting but also a carefully researched and accurately depicted visual history of the evolution of navigation. Ironically, Millet, who passionately loved ships, perished in the *Titanic* disaster in 1912.

MODERN SHIPBUILDING AND REPAIRING

Apremier port must have large, superior ship repair facilities. Baltimore is fortunate in having two—Bethlehem Steel Corporation's Upper & Lower Yards, and the Maryland Shipbuilding & Drydock Company.

The history of what is now the Bethlehem's Upper Yard begins over a century ago with William Skinner, a native of Dorchester County where he had learned shipbuilding as applied to brigs, barks and schooners. In 1820 he arrived in Baltimore and sharpened his skills in the shipyards of Fells Point. In 1827 he established his own yard at the foot of Henry Street in Federal Hill. By 1845, the demand for sailing craft and bay steamboats had become great enough to encourage expanding in a new location at the foot of Cross Street, present site of the Upper Yard.

Skinner Dry Dock #2, Upper Yard

Henry F. Rinn

With the Civil War came an unparalleled demand for new sailing vessels, and of course, tremendous prosperity for the shipbuilding industry. By 1866 the United States Navy was considered as great or greater than any other fleet.

It was not long, however, before the wartime Navy began to deteriorate. American business interest had shifted from the coast to the interior, following what was to be the usual trend of post-war economics. It was not until about 1880 that the United States began to initiate an ambitious shipbuilding and repair program. Presidents Garfield and Arthur deserved much of the credit for starting a maritime revival. Under the ownership of Columbian Iron Works, the Fort McHenry graving dock was built in 1880—site of the present Lower Yard. Today this facility is considered to be the first modern graving dock in the country.

In 1887 the Columbian Iron Works received a contract calling for the construction of an all-steel gunboat. The *USS Patrol* was launched October 13, 1888 and commissioned as part of Admiral Dewey's squadron. The second steel vessel to be built at the Lower Yard was the *Maverick,* owned by the Standard Oil Corporation. The *Maverick* was the first bulk oil tanker to be built in America and the largest all-steel ship built up to that time.

Argonaut, Lower Yard

Bethlehem Steel Company

The keel of the *Argonaut* was laid at the Lower Yard in 1896. It was an historical first because it was the first successful commercial submarine ever built, and is considered the forerunner of modern undersea research vessels. It was powered by a 30 HP internal combustion engine designed for 10 hours of continuous submergence. It had a length of 36 feet and was 9 feet wide. Air was supplied by a rubber hose suspended above the water's surface with buoys. The *Argonaut* traveled along the Bay's floor on three wheels and was used mainly for salvage work.

At the turn of the century, the Columbian Iron Works had an extremely successful business, but because of expansion difficulties, it went bankrupt and was bought by the Baltimore Shipbuilding & Drydock Company.

Both the Upper and Lower Yards were operated until business reverses brought

First shipyard at Sparrows Point   *Mary McIntyre*

about a reorganization in 1914. Receivership occurred the following year when Skinner had to relinquish control. In April, 1916, the Baltimore Shipbuilding & Drydock Company purchased both yards and operated them throughout World War I. On October 1, 1921, all the properties of the Baltimore Shipbuilding and Dry Dock Company were acquired by the Bethlehem Shipbuilding Corporation and the yards turned almost exclusively to repair work.

In 1916 Bethlehem acquired the Sparrows Point shipyard, formerly operated by the Maryland Steel Company.

In 1890 this shipbuilding yard was built as an adjunct to the steel works, an innovation in both the steel-making and shipbuilding industry. Within two years the yard was in operation. The tug boat *Pennwood* was its initial product, a hyphenated name for the Pennsylvania Steel Company and the plant's first manager, Frederick W. Wood. The tug was followed by the *Alabama, Raleigh* and the *Florida* for the Old Bay Line, and by the much larger *Gloucester* for the Merchants and Miners Transportation Company.

The integrated plants worked well together. The yard, even in its earliest days, was highly efficient.

In 1893, however, following a profitable year, the Sparrows Point plant produced less because of a national depression and the shipyard was closed for five years. But by 1898, sparked by the war with Spain, contracts were secured from the Navy for

Pennwood, first tugboat built at Sparrows Point

Maryland Historical Society

Thomas Booz and Brother Shipyard, Canton, about 1875. Steambox at center for softening planks, mold loft at right.

Peale Museum

the construction of three torpedo boat destroyers, and for several 6,000 ton and 13,000-ton cargo carriers.

In 1899 the yard began work on a large floating dry dock for the U.S. Naval Reservation. Its construction attracted national attention, especially its tow by two tugs for the 1,800-mile trip to New Orleans. In 1905 the largest floating dry dock in the world, the *Dewey,* was completed and towed to the Philippines. It was 500 feet long and 100 feet wide, capable of handling a vessel of about 19,000 deadweight tons.

On March 1, 1923, the 6,000 and 20,000-ton floating drydocks from Sparrows Point were moved to the Upper Yard. This was expanded by the acquisition of adjoining properties in 1926, 1930 and 1939. The final acquisition came about in 1941 with the absorption of the land formerly owned by the Redman and Vane Shipbuilding Company, Baltimore Ship Repair Company and Booz Brothers, Inc. Including land and water, Bethlehem Steel's Baltimore Yards now own 28.33 acres and have the use of 6.78 government-owned acres.

During World War II, Bethlehem's Upper and Lower yards were a frenzy of activity as merchant ships of every allied nation were repaired and improved before sailing through a hostile sea of German submarines and surface raiders. The installation of armorplate and gun platforms and magazines was carried out around the clock. Passenger liners were converted into troop transports for the Navy. At the same time, ships damaged by hostile action were under repair. Some 4,500 ships were repaired, reconditioned, or converted during the war. In addition the Government leased the Fairfield Shipyard to Bethlehem Steel Corporation which produced more vessels—384 new Liberty ships alone—than any other yard in the nation.

Bethlehem Steel's Lower Yard

Bethlehem Steel Company

Bethlehem Steel's Upper Yard

Bethlehem Steel Company

Since the war the Baltimore yards have again concentrated on repair work with more than 200 conversions and reconversions. There have been some notable exceptions. In 1966–67, they built the *Ridgely Warfield*, designed for the Underseas Research Department of Johns Hopkins University, the first all-aluminum research vessel.

The volume of work for shore installations has increased tremendously. Bethlehem now produces pre-fabricated steel buildings, hoppers, chutes, conveyors frames, and section barge hulls. The yards also are equipped for hammer and press forging, and have manufactured steam winches, steam and diesel foundations, and frames of all types.

The Maryland Shipbuilding and Drydock Company founded in 1922, is located on a 98-acre tract on the south bank of the Patapsco River. With complete facilities for ship construction, ship conversions and ship repair, it has one of the most modern and best equipped shipyards on the Atlantic seaboard.

During World War II the shipyard operated at peak efficiency, repairing every type of sea-going vessel, installing armorplate and gun platforms on allied vessels and converting passenger liners to troop transports.

The company has pursued a policy of continuous development and expansion. During the past ten years it has invested over $8,000,000 for additional facilities and new equipment. It can accommodate 30 ocean-going vessels simultaneously at five piers and in four drydocks. The largest of these drydocks, put in operation in 1967, is the second largest floating drydock on the East Coast capable of servicing vessels up to 775 feet long and 106 feet in beam, with a lifting capacity of 33,000 tons. The drydock has greatly enhanced the yard's conversion and repair potential and is attracting an increased flow of marine business.

The major specialty of the company has included the lengthening of tankers, deep sea passenger ferries and bulk carriers, and the conversion of ships to container carriers, multiple cargo tankers, bulk carriers, as well as the redesign and rebuilding of dredges.

The now famous, acclaimed process of "jumbo-izing" vessels was a product of the ingenuity of Maryland's engineering personnel. This is a method of increasing the carrying capacity of existing ships by as much as 50 percent. The unique process—whereby vessels are enlarged through the insertion of midbodies—has revolutionized ship renovation world wide. As the leader in this field, Maryland has perhaps done more ship enlarging than any other yard in the country.

Maryland Shipbuilding and Drydock Company's capabilities are not limited to standard ship repairs and conversion, but include prototypes in construction of unique vessels, which can be undertaken only in a yard with far-reaching ability.

This is illustrated in the construction of the 9,000-ton prototype for the U.S. Navy, designated T-AKD-1, and named *U.S.N.S. Point Barrow*. This is actually a small drydock, the first of a class of cargo ships whose summary mission is to service Arctic military bases.

The *H. S. Victoria* is a hydrofoil vessel of unique design built by Maryland for Northwest Hydrofoil Lines. The 65-foot boat was designed to "fly" commuters between Seattle and Victoria, British Columbia, with a capacity of 75 passengers.

In 1963, Maryland delivered to the Woods Hole Oceanographic Institution of Woods Hole, Massachusetts, the first American vessel designed and built specifically for oceanographic research. The *Atlantis II* is a floating laboratory, carrying scientists on their missions to explore the ocean floor. Because of her unique purpose, nearly every aspect of the design and construction of *Atlantis II* required special consideration.

Maryland Shipbuilding & Drydock Co.   *Maryland Shipbuilding & Drydock Co.*

She is now efficiently performing an important service in furthering man's knowledge of the sea.

Maryland's Industrial Products Division designs, manufactures and installs large steam surface condensers for the electric utility industry, as well as pressure vessels, evaporators, and a wide variety of heavy industrial machined components and structural steel.

In an active shipbuilding center such as ours, it was inevitable that new and sometimes revolutionary building designs should be tried. Some were important in that they sought to meet local needs, as did the old mud machines first used for dredging the harbor, and the first ice breakers when freezing occurred.

Two of the strangest craft ever built here were Ross Winans' Cigar Ship and the *Howard Cassard*.

Ross Winans, whose object it was "to advance the science of commerce by supplying vessels which will more fully answer the requirements than any heretofore constructed," began construction of his novel cigar vessel in 1858. His reasons were:

"With a view to obtain greater safety, dispatch, uniformity, and certainty, as well as economy of transportation by sea, we devised and combined the elements exhibited in the vessel in question.

"Experience has shown that steam-power on board sea-going vessels, when used in aid of sails, insures, to a great extent dispatch, certainty of action, and uniformity in time of their voyages. Now we believe that by discarding sails entirely and all their necessary appendages, the building of the vessel of iron, having reference to the use of steam alone, those most desirable ends may be even still more fully obtained.

"The length of the vessel I am building is more than eleven times its breadth of beam, being sixteen feet broad and one hundred and eighty feet long."

Around this huge cigar-shaped iron vessel at midship was an iron wheel with flanges at an angle, adapted to propel the vessel. The wheel was driven by machinery from inside the hull, and was covered by a belt of iron broad enough to enclose it. Four high-pressure engines supplied the motive-power.

This nondescript ship was launched in October, 1858 at Winans' shipyard at Port Covington, about where the Western Maryland Railway's grain elevator now stands. The vessel made an unsatisfactory trial trip in January, 1859 to North Point and back, attaining an average speed of about twelve miles per hour. Experimental trials during the next six months induced Winans to increase her length to 219 feet. In December, 1859 the vessel went to Norfolk and from there made several experimental trips to sea, returning to Baltimore December 12, again without meeting the inventor's expectations. Winans spent over $2,000,000 before abandoning the project.

The Cassards were a wealthy Baltimore family, accumulating a fortune in the lard trade. Howard Cassard, head of the family, was approached by Robert M. Freyer

Cigar Ship   *Maryland Historical Society*

Howard Cassard

Mariners Museum, Newport News, Va.

who sought backing for a plan to construct a steamship designed to cross the Atlantic in half the time required by the large liners. Freyer, as any shipyard laborer might know by examining his plans, was not a naval architect, but then neither was Howard Cassard who accepted the designer's salespitch, thereby sealing the doom of a large part of his ready cash.

As if to compound Freyer's lack of familiarity with nautical matters, the firm of H. Ashton Ramsey, who were not shipwrights, were selected to build the ship. The workers of Ramsey's Federal Hill plant, with the exception of a few riveters, had never before even repaired a ship. It is not known whether either Freyer or Cassard tried to interest any of the competent Baltimore shipbuilders in accepting the contract, but it is probable that no reputable shipyard would have touched it.

The *Howard Cassard* was to be a sort of seagoing Pullman. She was 222 feet in length, with an 18-foot depth of keel, but her beam was only sixteen feet. Making her float would be a task akin to making a board float edgewise in the water. To compensate for his hull's inherent instability afloat, Freyer designed a cast iron keel of 34 tons. The *Cassard* was also to carry 80,000 pounds of machinery and 200,000 pounds of coal. Her propeller shaft was 92 feet long (said to be the largest forging made up to its time) and displaced sixteen tons.

Being too narrow to allow for staterooms, the *Cassard* was fitted with Pullman-style berths. Externally, she was a rather good-looking ship (if viewed broadside), having the appearance of a large yacht, with a clipper bow and short bowsprit, three masts and two stacks. There was no other superstructure except skylights, a fiddlen and a pilothouse.

The launching of this remarkable vessel was set for November 6, 1890. George Kelly, a recognized expert in such matters, had been approached to supervise the launch, but had declined. Freyer then undertook to handle the matter himself. With 5,000 spectators gathered on the shore, and more watching from the decks of the excursion steamer *Columbia,* 11-year-old Alice Freyer broke a bottle of champagne across the bow. The tripping blocks were hammered away, but the *Cassard* stood fast. The tug *Parole* tried to start her down the ways, but the tow line parted.

Not discouraged, Freyer rescheduled the launching for the following day, and many of the spectators returned. This time, the tug *Britannia* passed the *Cassard* a line and she began at last to move toward the water. When the ways parted, she began to list to starboard. The list increased due to the shifting of her coal and her mast struck the tug *Baltimore,* carrying away the tug's smokestack and flagstaff. Having lost two of her three masts in this encounter, the *Cassard* now floated in the Basin with an extreme list. She was righted and towed to Woodall's shipyard for repairs.

With repairs completed, a trial trip was scheduled and a number of guests were invited. They started off stalwartly, but had travelled only a short distance when the *Cassard* began once again to list alarmingly whereupon the passengers became panicky and demanded to be put ashore. This only voyage of the *Howard Cassard* covered a distance of about one mile. Twelve idle years later, she was sold for scrap for $1,775.

In the middle 1940's, Bethlehem did an unusual refitting project on the *Sea Cloud,* an ocean-going yacht belonging to Mrs. Marjorie Post Davies that cost a million dollars to build in 1931. The engineers and draftsmen had to prepare a complete new set of plans to do the work. She was 350 feet long and required a crew of 72.

Sea Cloud, at Baltimore Yards

Bethlehem Steel Company

THE TRAGEDY OF THE "ALUM CHINE"

THE BRITISH TRAMP steamer *Alum Chine* arrived in Baltimore March 1, 1913, anchoring in the Patapsco River opposite Hawkins Point to load dynamite for Colon, Panama. The dynamite was to be used in excavating the Panama Canal. Ten carloads were shipped from Delaware and on arrival in Canton were placed on barges to be loaded on the ship.

Seven carloads of dynamite were loaded on Wednesday, March 5, and two on Thursday, leaving one to be loaded Friday. The loading was expected to be finished by 10 AM as the vessel had been set up to sail at noon. Customs officials had inspected the loading at 9 AM and left on the cutter *Guthrie* to meet another vessel. About the same time the tug *Atlantic* set out to pick up the barge on which the stevedores were working.

The *Guthrie* had been away from the vessel about an hour and was returning up the Patapsco, when those on board noticed fire in the forward part of the *Alum Chine. Guthrie's* crew realized the danger. They threw up the windows of the boat in preparation for the explosion which they felt was bound to come and started full speed toward the *Alum Chine*. In that few minutes there was a tremendous roar—a roar that had never been heard in the harbor before. The *Guthrie* leaped from the water, swayed from side to side and plunged upward and downward before recovering.

A blinding flash and a tongue of flame shot 200 feet in the air. Fragments of iron and steel were hurled skyward as if by some preternatural, catapultic force.

The fragments of the steel and iron, many of them four and five feet in height went hurling through the air, falling like showers of meteors on the decks of the collier *Jason*, a quarter of a mile away. The *Jason*, recently built for the U. S. Government by the Maryland Steel Company, had just returned from her trial trip, a trim vessel, beautiful and sharply rigged. She was raked from bow to stern by the heavy missiles which killed or injured those on board. The cabin and the officers' quarters were crushed and battered, lifeboats were splintered and the sides of the ship punctured.

The spectacular explosion was followed by a cloud of dense smoke, which quickly settled. All the *Guthrie's* crew could see was the burning tug *Atlantic*. Captain J. R. Dunn, of the *Guthrie,* went full speed to the scene. His brother, Captain Alonzo Dunn, of the tug *Britannia,* Captain Owen W. Thompson, of the tug *Curtis Bay,* and the captain of the tug *Mary P. Riehl* heard the explosion and started from different parts of the harbor for the scene of the accident.

The heroism of Captain Van Dyke and Mate Diggs of the tug *Atlantic* formed the most touching chapter of the whole tragedy. When the fire broke out many of the crew of the *Alum Chine* had been saved by James Goodhues and his brother Jerome in their launch which was near the scene. The Captain of *Atlantic,* having saved, as

The Alum Chine explosion

Baltimore Sunpapers

he thought, all of those on board the vessel and the barge, gave orders to put about. As he was pulling away from the doomed steamer two men appeared on the bow, screaming for help.

Captain Van Dyke and Mate Diggs knew what it meant to turn about, but they did. After taking the two men off, the tug started to back away. But it was too late. There was a sudden roar and the tug was caught in a maelstrom of fire. The captain and mate were scalded to death, and the tug became a floating fire brand.

The Goodhues brothers and the captains of the *Mary P. Riehl* and the *Britannia* aided in saving some of those on board the blazing tug and from the water where some had leaped. The *Britannia* tried to tow the *Atlantic* to shore, but she sank a few yards from the *Alum Chine*.

The tugs rushed the injured and dying to Baltimore where they were met by doctors and ambulances. In all 27 were killed and 67 injured. The casualties would have been higher had it not been for brave men on the launch and tugs who risked their own lives to save others.

The explosion shook houses along the eastern section of Baltimore county as well as in northeastern and southern parts of the city. Windows were broken and houses tottered as if moved by an earthquake. Sparrows Point and Curtis Bay especially, felt the shock. The heavy iron doors in the barracks at Fort Howard and Fort Carroll shook on their hinges.

Earth tremors from the shock were felt in a number of cities and towns in Maryland, Pennsylvania, New Jersey and Delaware. In Dover, Delaware, a session of the legislature was interrupted; the Speaker of the House remarked that "there must have been an earthquake somewhere."

On May 2, 1913 H. G. Harper & Company of Cardiff, England, owners of the *Alum Chine,* presented gold cigarette cases to James and Jerome Goodhues for their heroic conduct in saving life at the risk of their own, and they also received gold watches from the British Government. Later they were nominated for the Carnegie Medal of Honor. The first question Carnegie investigators asked James Goodhues was, "Would you do it again?" He replied, "Hell No." And that ended the interview and the chance for the medal.

MARYLAND PORT ADMINISTRATION: 1956–1982

BY 1950 IT became apparent that a coordinating, controlling authority would have to be established to combine the growing number of agencies and groups engaged in port operations. A Port of Baltimore Commission was organized to provide more liberalized loans for port improvements than had been provided by the State Act of 1920. In 1956 the General Assembly enacted legislation establishing the Maryland Port Authority, a single agency which would coordinate the efforts of city, state and private groups on behalf of Maryland's ports.

"The members of the Maryland Port Authority met for the purpose of organizing on June 14, 1956, at 11:15 A.M. in the Governor's office at 10 Light Street in the City of Baltimore, Maryland."

—From Minute Book, Maryland Port Authority

Attending the meeting were the five commissioners who had been appointed to supervise its policies and programs: Robert Williams, representing Baltimore City; Paul R. Smith, Western Maryland; Avery W. Hall, the Eastern Shore; Edward S. Corcoran, Anne Arundel County; D. Luke Hopkins, Baltimore County. Also attending were Joseph L. Stanton, executive director of the Maryland Port Authority, and James W. Davis, secretary.

Early in its existence the Port Authority recognized that certain fundamental approaches would be necessary to reach its stated goals. Briefly stated, they were:

1—Policies and programs must be carried out by an experienced and knowledgeable staff who were career-oriented, and with freedom to carry out responsibilities limited only by good judgment and professional standards.

2—The physical condition of the port was such that it would not be sufficient to simply repair, improve or add to present facilities. An aggressive overall modernization program was needed. The Authority would be the instrument for creating this new port of Baltimore.

3—Port policies and practices had been heavily influenced by the railroads serving the port through their ownership of most port facilities. To capture additional cargo, the port would have to improve its competitive position and be turned from a railroad to a shippers' port.

4—While moving toward a leadership role in development and promotion of the port. the Authority would be keenly conscious at all times of its legislative command to assist and promote private industry. A cooperative partnership must be formed between the public and private agencies in the joint development and promotion of the port.

An agreement covering the transfer of waterfront properties and port operations from the City of Batlimore to the Maryland Port Authority was completed on August 14, 1957. It covered the transfer of the McComas Street Terminal of the Western Maryland Railway, the National Gypsum Company Pier, and the Recreation Pier from city ownership to the Port Authority.

The Authority took over such harbor functions as maintenance dredging, ice breaking, operation of the city's marine radio station, scavenger work, conducting surveys, issuing of permits, carrying on of inspections, and similar maritime duties that in the past had been performed by the Bureau of Harbors.

In its first five years the Authority had been engaged in assembling a staff, gathering data on the port and its needs and laying out its program priorities. The first priority was a deeper and wider channel leading into Baltimore to accommodate the increasing size of ocean-going vessels. This is dealt with in the chapter on dredging.

Hawkins Point

Maryland Port Administration

Since the Port Authority was, by law, instructed to assist private industry in the expansion and modernization of its facilities, it was natural that the first major construction project undertaken was the rebuilding of a pier on behalf of the Baltimore & Ohio Railroad. The pier, which had been used during World War II for loading of ammunition, had suffered severe fire damage and for many years remained unused.

The pier was on Hawkins Point, the northernmost segment of a parcel of property called Marley Neck. It had been described as the finest remaining waterfront industrial development area of the East Coast.

Area business and civic leaders, as well as the B & O, brought about a rezoning of the area for heavy industry. One of the pioneer developers was the Kennecott Refining Corporation. As part of the inducement to Kennecott to locate in the area, the B & O agreed to provide pier facilities capable of importing blister copper and exporting finished copper products.

The railroad, in turn, asked the Port Authority to construct the pier. The B & O was to turn over the remains of the old pier plus substantial backup areas, and the Authority would construct the new pier and lease all of it to the railroad.

Construction was completed in 1958 at a cost of more than $3,000,000. The funding was a combination of general obligation and revenue bonds secured by a lease between the Authority and the railroad. It was a two-berth, open-finger pier with rail tracks on the apron and supports for future installation of cranes. A 38-foot channel was dredged from the main ship channel and necessary appurtenances were constructed.

In 1959 the Authority purchased from the city a 356-acre tract which had been the municipal airport, Harbor Field. This was far more than a simple acquisition of prime waterfront property. It opened the way for the Authority's major expansion program, providing a uniquely suited site for the construction of terminal facilities that met the most modern criteria and design. Of equal importance, this Dundalk Marine Terminal gave the Authority an opportunity to carry out under commercial stress its long-proposed policies of equal rates for all users and equal access for all forms of water and land transportation.

Harbor Field which was to become the Dundalk Marine Terminal   *Maryland Port Administration*

The first contracts for repairing existing buildings, fencing a storage area for import automobiles, dredging access channels and rebuilding bulkheads were under way by May 20, 1959.

From its beginnings Dundalk has been used as a terminal for imported automobiles. This began in 1956 with 8,000 cars, mostly Volkswagens. The following year the number had risen to 22,534, and by 1971 it had reached 314,850. This was the port's biggest year, and the record was reached in ten months because of a two-month longshoremen's strike. Port officials believe in twelve months the terminal would have handled 60,000 more, which would have given Baltimore a record for American ports. Automobile imports have not been as high in recent years because of changes in the automobile business and the recession in the early '80's. Today more than 250,000 cars arrive annually both at the Dundalk Marine Terminal and Atlantic Terminals near Fairfield.

The major work of converting the terminal from an airfield to a modern marine cargo-handling center was covered in six related construction phases. When this was finished, in July, 1967, eight marginal berths had been provided, four high-speed gantry cranes were in service, and four new transit sheds and one warehouse had been erected.

The phases were continuous, and, in some cases, almost overlapping as the cargo demand for the terminal facilities increased at a phenomenal rate. This program, starting at such modest levels in 1959, had reached a level of expenditure of $25,000,000 by 1967. In 1967, the terminal cargo volume reached the 1,000,000 ton mark. In effect, the construction program and cargo flow had been running a head-to-head race.

Dundalk Marine Terminal

Maryland Port Administration

Locust Point, North Side
Maryland Port Administration

On New Year's Day, 1964, the Maryland Port Authority took possession of the historic Locust Point Marine Terminal through a long-term lease agreement. For more than a century the facility had been owned and operated by the B & O. Though it was still the largest single cargo center in the port, the piers, once the pride of the B & O, were in an advanced stage of decay. It was the condition of these piers and the inability of the railroad to underwrite the urgently-needed renovation and expansion that had been a prime factor in the decision of the railroad to turn over the facility to the Authority.

The railroad leased Locust Point to the Authority for 40 years at $1 per year with a 40-year renewal option. The Authority also received purchase rights. In return for the token rental, the Authority agreed to make capital improvements and to honor the railroad's exclusive rights to provide all rail service to the terminal.

The Authority's program at Locust Point was based on two components— substantial emergency maintenance and repair projects, and a program for turning the obsolete piers into up-to-date cargo-handling facilities. Within two years the maintenance program had been completed. The Authority had expended almost $1,000,000 in repairing roofs, decks of piers, removing surface structures and completing a sweeping housekeeping operation.

The finger pier configuration was maintained because replacement with marginal pier facilities would be excessively costly, and would reduce the number of berths below acceptable minimals.

Originally, the plans called for the construction of three new berth complexes— Berth 3, Berths 4–5 and Berths 9–10, along with the renovation of Berth 6. In the first revision of the master plan, the decision was made to eliminate the 9–10 complex because of a lack of backup areas to support such a facility.

The new Pier 3 facility was completed in September, 1966 and leased to Lavino Shipping Company. This modern, two-berth facility featured an unusual truck-rail apron arrangement on the rear platform of the shed that increased efficiency with marginal flow of traffic into a finger pier. The $4,000,000 investment handles tonnage well beyond the capacity of its predecessor.

The second major project on the north side of Locust Point was the rebuilding of the Pier 4 and 5 site. The new facility was opened in March, 1970 with a two-berth, open pier served by high-speed gantry cranes in combination with a large transit shed pier for both berths.

While no major structural changes were made to Piers 6 & 8, the facilities were upgraded by repairs and the installation of new elevators. In further negotiations with the B & O, the Authority was able to secure an additional eleven acres to support the new installations.

After the B & O turned over its Locust Point facility to the Authority, the Pennsylvania Railroad also decided that, as a common carrier, it should concentrate on freight traffic rather than the operation of piers. In December, 1967, the Authority acquired the general cargo facilities of the Pennsylvania Railroad, known as Pier 1 and Pier 6, Clinton Street, and 14 acres of property for open storage.

Pier 6 was an older pier of limited use in recent years because of substructure deterioration. For a number of years it served as a registration hall for longshoremen, and at the present it is being used for limited storage, barge tie-up and other services.

The principal acquisition was Pier 1—a four-berth, doubledeck facility in excellent structural condition. To provide for increased truck traffic a ramp bridging Clinton Street from a paved backup to the pier's second deck was constructed. This enabled Atlantic & Gulf Stevedoring Company, the lease holder, to have quick dispatch

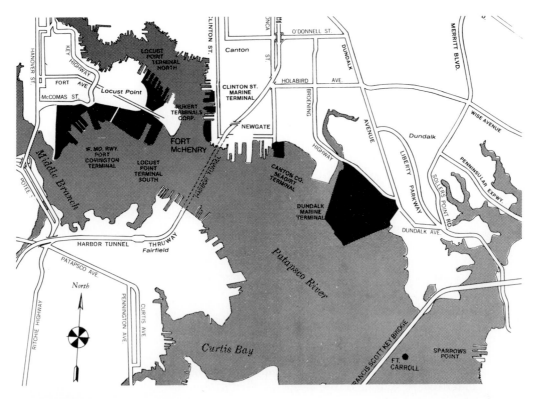

Map of Harbor   *Maryland Port Administration*

of truck traffic from both decks of the pier.

In 1969 a major industry was seeking an East Coast site. It required proximity to a deepwater port where raw materials could be imported and finished products exported. Cooperative efforts by the Maryland Port Authority, the B & O, the Potomac Edison Company and the Maryland Department of Economic Development concluded with Howmet-Pechiney subletting from the B & O the pier facility at Hawkins Point. Howmet-Pechiney installed a high-speed conveyor and storage system for the transfer of raw alumina from vessels to special rail cars. The cars then moved the alumina 40 miles to the site of a new Eastalco aluminum plant built by Howmet-Pechiney near Frederick, Maryland. The improvements to the pier were so designed as to protect the movement of Kennecott products and other commodities.

Though it was one of the Authority's smaller projects, Hawkins Point, the first endeavor of the Authority, has proven to be a textbook example of a port facility that has created substantially increased industrial wealth for the state.

The critical need for additional space on the northside of Locust Point to support the new cargo-handling facilities resulted in a chain of events leading to the Authority's acquisition of the B & O's remaining waterfront property on the southside of Locust Point. When the Authority asked the railroad to sell or lease acreage to supply the northside pier backup area, the railroad requested that negotiations be expanded to include transfer of undeveloped property on the southside of Locust Point, and the fruit pier built by the railroad and operated by the United Fruit Company. Thus began a series of negotiations involving the Authority, the B & O, United Fruit and the Western Maryland Railway, which was asked to give up control of some of its space on the southside to open the way for a major construction program.

Seagirt, Baltimore's first container operation.

In July, 1970, negotiations were concluded. The Authority purchased eleven acres of backup area on the northside and a parcel of land on the southside, including the fruit pier leased to the United Fruit Company. This, with the Western Maryland property, comprised a site suitable for the development of a new, modern marginal cargo handling terminal.

In 1970, the Maryland General Assembly created a cabinet-level State Department of Transportation, which became operational on July 1, 1971. The semiautonomous Maryland Port Authority, redesignated as the Maryland Port Administration, was one of seven formerly individual State agencies absorbed by the new department.

On June 25, 1971, the Commissioners of the Maryland Port Authority met for the last time. For a period of fifteen years, an organization unique in the history of the State had carried out a special legislative mandate promulgated by the 1956 Maryland General Assembly. The Maryland Port Authority in a decade and-a-half did an outstanding task in launching and carrying out a bold new maritime program for the port.

The first order of business for the new Maryland Port Administration was to upgrade its existing facilities to handle the new method of shipping cargo-containers.

Containerization, which has revolutionized water carrier transportation, was the idea of Malcolm McLean, president of McLean Transportation, a successful trucking company. McLean, a legend in his own time, was convinced that a way could be discovered to combine the economy of water transportation with the speed and flexibility of overland shipment. His first plan was a roll-on, roll-off operation with the chassis and box remaining intact. Now this was not new. It had been tried and found wanting in two areas in the early fifties. A trailer ferry service was inaugurated after the war to haul units from New York City to Albany, N.Y., and return, but it failed. A few years later, this same concept was used in a service from New York to Jacksonville, Florida, but this too proved unworkable.

It was during McLean's efforts to acquire Interstate Commerce Commission certification that his thinking changed. Rather than ro-ro, he would employ the same method used for centuries of lifting up - over - and down, however, he could see the practicality of lifting the entire truck body off the chassis and stowing it. He had no knowledge of ocean shipping, but what he conceived required a far greater knowledge of trucking than ship operation. He believed the container vessel to be nothing more than a "glorified ferryboat."

McLean purchased a T-2 tanker and supervised its conversion for container carriage and was aboard the "Ideal X," when a test run was taken. He was aware of the many rebuffs directed at the new concept, mainly from American flag ship-owners. Some naval architects questioned the ability of the converted tanker, with its 58 containers on deck, to withstand heavy seas. Soon after commencing a coastwise service the vessel was to go through hurricane waters without incident. Growth came quickly. With the purchase of Pan-Atlantic Steamship Corporation, a subsidiary of Waterman Steamship Corporation, McLean became the owner of seven C-2 type cargo carriers. Having proven to himself that the movement of containers by vessels was practical, he took another great step. Taking one of his C-2 vessels, the *Gateway City,* he had it converted to the first fully containerized vessel, capable of carrying 226 trailers. This child of containerization was to grow into a service soon to become known as Sea-Land Service, Inc., which would change ocean transportation.

The port's first direct containership service began on April 9, 1963, with the arrival of the *Mobile* at Pier 10, Canton Marine Terminal, the first area designed for containerized freight. The *Mobile* and her sistership, the *New Orleans,* operated a Baltimore to Puerto Rico container run for Sea-Land Service, Inc.

Locust Point, South Side   *Maryland Port Administration*

The success of this operation encouraged Sea-Land and the Canton Company to begin construction in 1965 of Baltimore's first specialized containership terminal in the Sea Girt area. By 1966, what had begun as a trickle of container traffic was growing to a torrent.

While many of the ports comprising the North Atlantic range hesitated, awaiting further developments, the Maryland Port Administration completed its own containership studies. It moved to provide a site where massive amounts of container cargo could be transferred, and where expansion to meet projected increasing future demands could be accomplished. The site chosen was Dundalk Marine Terminal.

Initially, two existing berths were adapted to accommodate containers, and existing 50-ton gantry cranes were fitted with spreaders, pending construction of a high bridge type Paceco crane with a 40-ton capacity. Four new container berths were constructed, two in 1971 and two in 1973, each served by a new Paceco crane. The main thrust of Maryland Port Administration planning was to develop Dundalk into the facility capable of handling an anticipated burgeoning container trade.

The wisdom of Baltimore's commitment to containerization, manifested in the development of Dundalk, can be seen in the huge tonnage increases in the terminal's container traffic in the first five years. In 1968, 77,455 tons of container freight were handled and this increased each year until 1972 when 1,230,000 tons passed through the terminal.

Cooperation between the public and private sectors of the maritime community was demonstrated when the port's three huge grain elevators were taken over by large grain companies. The Indiana Farm Bureau Cooperative Association, Inc. acquired the B & O elevator in 1970, the Central Soya Company the Pennsylvania Railroad elevator in 1971, and the Louis Dreyfus Corporation the Western Maryland Railway elevator in 1974. The three companies have invested millions of dollars in improvements over the past five years.

Except for 1977, when 4,840,000 tons moved throughout the port, grain exports have exceeded 5 million tons each year since, peaking at 5,990,000 tons in 1979. Barring unexpected developments in world politics, or a crop disaster in the Midwest, the 6,000,000 tons mark could be reached by the port in 1982 or 1983. Each ton of grain moving through the port results in some $10.50 in direct economic benefits.

In 1963 the Maryland Port Administration decided the port should have an appropriate symbol of its stature as a major factor in maritime commerce, and that such a symbol might best take the form of a World Trade Center. It would house the major administrative officers of the MPA and become a focal point for Baltimore's waterfront-related business, with ample space for consular offices and other firms associated with the foreign commerce and shipping industry.

Construction of a 30-story, pentagonally-shaped World Trade Center started in June, 1972, after razing the ancient building on Pier 2 Pratt Street, which for 20 years housed the staff of the MPA. Completed in early 1977, at a cost of $21,000,000, the building, rising 423 feet above the waters of the Inner Harbor, contains some 313,000 square feet of office space. It also houses advanced communications facilities to serve its international maritime clientele including a computerized information bank linked to Interfile, data transmission services, multi-lingual secretarial services and the World Trade Institute.

Even though it had been operating for a few months, the Southside Locust Point Terminal was officially opened on April 30, 1979. The dedication, held inside the 120,000 square-foot consolidation shed at the terminal, was sponsored jointly by the Maryland Port Administration and Atlantic and Gulf Stevedores, Inc. which has a five year contract to operate the terminal owned by the MPA.

"Our action in leasing this terminal is a firm indication of the direction we intend to follow in future port development," W. Gregory Halpin, Maryland Port Administrator said, "looking more and more toward letting the private sector play a larger role in port operations."

The two-and-a-half berth terminal has 37 acres of backup space, equipped with two container cranes, one 330-ton heavy lift crane and one 100 Whirly crane.

The contract for building the last container berth at Dundalk Marine Terminal was awarded in 1980. Completion is scheduled for 1982. When finished it will have thirteen berths, ten cranes and 545 acres of backup space, making it one of the finest, if not the finest, container terminals in the United States.

Adding to the port's container cargo capabilities is the vast and diverse rail network provided by three trunkline systems, and one of the largest interstate motor concentrations of over 160 lines. Together they expedite inbound and outbound container traffic at cost-saving rates. Portwide, virtually every service necessary to conveniently and efficiently move containerized freight is readily available.

It took fourteen years to move a million containers through the port following the first direct containership service in 1963. This milestone occurred in January, 1977. The second million, in contrast, took only four years because of continuing development of container trade, modern facilities and other port improvements. Handling these 2,000,000 containers has resulted in an estimated $773,000,000 increase to the Maryland economy.

A record total of 4,600,000 tons of container cargo moved through the port in 1980, making Baltimore the second largest in container cargo volume among all Atlantic and Gulf Coast ports.

The port aims to maintain its leadership in containerization with future developments. In 1978 the Maryland Port Administration purchased the Masonville property on the southwest branch of the Patapsco River. This consisted of 126 acres, and when bulkheaded out to the Port Warden line and filled, the site will contain 350 acres. Dredging for a new tunnel under the Baltimore Harbor is generating a large amount of earth material that is being placed behind a bulkhead as fill in the Seagirt area. When completed the site will consist of 115 acres with 4200 feet of marginal pier space. Plans are for both areas to be developed into container and general cargo facilities.

To promote the port, the Maryland Port Administration maintains a worldwide network of trade development offices. In addition to a staff in Baltimore, it has national offices in New York, Chicago and Pittsburgh, and overseas ones in London, Brussels, Tokyo and Hong Kong.

A unique city and port promotion, sponsored by the city and business interests, is the *Pride of Baltimore,* an authentic clipper ship. It was built with city funds—on the edge of the Inner Harbor—as a way of explaining an important part of Baltimore's maritime history, as well as enhancing the new port of Baltimore.

The *Pride* was launched on February 27, 1977. At the launching, Mayor William Donald Schafer declared, "During the years and months ahead, the *Pride of Baltimore* will be a goodwill ambassador from the city of Baltimore to other towns and cities along the Chesapeake, the Eastern and Gulf Coasts, and possibly Europe. She will carry with her, I am certain, the good wishes of all Baltimoreans as well as to symbolize many of the things for which our city can be proud. *Pride of Baltimore* will be a tribute to its port, its shipbuilding industry, magnificent redevelopment of our city, and the sense of determination of all Baltimoreans to preserve the important

Pride of Baltimore

Baltimore Promotion Council

traditions of our past . . ."

Since then the *Pride* has sailed more than 100,000 miles to 103 ports of call, carrying Baltimore's message to Europe, the Caribbean, Gulf of Mexico and the Great Lakes. In the summer of 1982 it traveled through the Panama Canal to the West Coast.

In the late 1970's Rukert Terminals were dealt a severe blow when the Interstate Division announced it would take over 75 percent of the company's operations and facilities at Lazaretto for five years during the construction of the new harbor tunnel. The loss included Berth A, transit sheds, offices and six acres of backup space. The agreement stipulated that Rukert Terminals must be out of the Lazaretto property by November 1, 1930. This required acquiring six acres, building a new office, four warehouses and a new 450-foot extension of the pier at its Clinton Street Terminal.

After months of negotiating Rukert Terminals purchased six acres on the east side of its Clinton Street Terminal from the Consolidated Rail Corporation. The new complex was finished during Christmas week, 1980, and is one of the port's finest operational terminal units. The success of this difficult task of relocation was only made possible by the full cooperation of the Interstate Division and the City of Baltimore.

On August 26, 1980 Rukert Terminals was notified by the Consolidation Coal Company that it had purchased the Cottman crane pier from The Canton Company and the pier would be converted into a coal-loading facility within one year. This created a serious problem since Cottman had unloaded all the imported bulk commodities consigned to Rukert Terminals for more than 50 years. It also unloaded all the street salt and ores for other local industries. No other crane pier was available in the Canton area.

Rukert Terminals finally decided to purchase a new bulk unloading crane to be installed at its Clinton Street Terminal at a cost of $2,500,000. The new installation was completed on May 4, 1982 in time to unload the M/V *Lago Peten Itza* with 6,000 tons of bulk urea.

THE MEN ON THE DOCKS: 1752–1982

LTHOUGH WE KNOW little about the first longshoremen in Baltimore, it is obvious that their work was essential. Arriving ships were anxiously watched for, their coming heralded by beacons ablaze on hilltops, the pealing of church bells, the firing of cannon—signals that alerted merchants and ships' chandlers. Criers strode the streets, sometimes with bells, sometimes with wooden clappers, announcing the ship and calling for "Men along the shore!" And the men, leaving their regular occupations, hurried to the piers hoping to earn a few English pence.

As commerce grew, longshoring gradually ceased to be a part-time occupation for men hastily called from their plows or blacksmith shops. The docking and sailing of ships became so frequent that longshoring assumed the character of regular work.

Pay day for the longshoremen, 1905

Library of Congress

They acquired skill and tricks in the special stowing of a hundred different cargoes, but their principal work—at first—was the tough job of loading hogshead of tobacco. It required a particularly rugged class of men. Not only was all cargo "bulled" by manual strength, but the type of products stowed aboard were especially heavy and cumbersome.

Up to the early 1900's the day began before dawn. Longshoremen gathered in the early darkness, forming a half-circle in front of the pier. The hiring boss—sometime speaking, sometime merely flicking his hand—chose the gang for the next shift, replacing a gang that had been working since sunset. The men were paid in cash and usually at dockside taverns.

The pre-dawn shape-up is no longer a common sight. Its disappearance is only one of the many changes that have altered the life and work in the port in recent years.

In May, 1908 the International Longshoremen Assocation established its first local in New York city. During the spring of 1913, Anthony Chlopek, then president of ILA, came to Baltimore and organized a white and black local. Within a few months he was successful in signing individual contracts with four of the largest stevedoring companies: Dresel, Rauschenberg and Company, Atlantic Transport Co., Robert Ramsey Co., and Joseph R. Foard Co. Both the ILA and the Industrial Workers of the World (Wobblies) were on the docks of Baltimore during World War I, but by 1917 the ILA had practical control.

The ILA's constitution declares in part, "We recognize that ability makes the man and not wealth or social distinction. We recognize no nationality or creed..." During the 1920's this principle had become daily practice on the Baltimore docks. While perfection may not have been attained, the longshore unions of Baltimore handled minority problems with intelligence, sanity and good will. In no American port was there such an imperative sense of speed, time pressure and endless activity.

The Steamship Trade Association of Baltimore, Inc. was organized to establish a rapport between labor and management, to maintain harmony for the betterment of the community and foster the general welfare of the port. Walter P. Coria, Charles E. Scarlett and William G. Walsh drafted the certificate of incorporation, certified on January 14, 1929.

It was founded during an era of ocean shipping far different from today. Vessels of 7,500 tons capacity with a speed of 7 knots were considered the finest ships engaged in world commerce. The only piece of mechanical equipment automotive in nature was the pull tractor which hauled iron-wheeled wagons around the docks. An iron-wheeled hand-truck, which itself weighed about 200 pounds, but could be more than a half-ton when loaded, was used extensively. It moved cargoes from dockside sometimes directly to within the holds of vessels through sideport operation. Cargo to be high-piled when discharged required physical handling to point of rest, then stacking beyond man height through muscular strength alone. The cargo hook, which no good longshoremen would be without, was the badge of the dockworkers. Inclement weather did not stop work. The men continued until there was a threat of damage to the cargo itself; even then rain tents were rigged to permit uninterrupted flow. The base wage rate in 1929 was 85¢ per hour without guarantees or fringe benefits, such as exist today. A man worked an hour and received the 85¢ in cash. Availability of work on the waterfront was as scarce as it was in other areas and the numbers seeking work were large.

Under these circumstances, the Association had little to do. Such was the demand for work that conditions were not a factor. If one man refused to work under

Longshoremen, with cargo hook and hand truck

A. Aubrey Bodine

duress, many others more were willing to take over. Harmony between the parties was simply the subject of work. There were no differences to settle. This period is perhaps best expressed by citing the slow upward movement of the base wage. It took ten years to reach the level of $1.05 per hour. Even this was reluctantly granted. The base wage on coastwise and intercoastal remained at 95¢ per hour for almost eight years.

Those conditions existed during the Depression and war years. Then with new opportunities, the longshore leadership moved to improve the wages and conditions of their members. At that time the union was headed by two of the most capable labor leaders in the history of the port: Jefferson Davis, International Vice President of the ILA, and August Idzik, Atlantic Coast District Vice President.

Jefferson Davis, an outstanding black union leader, was held in high regard by the stevedoring companies. It was Mr. Davis who was the "cement" holding things together when the going got rough during labor negotiations. He realized that outrageous demands of some radical workmen was an affront to the employers and he was quick to modify them. He became known throughout the union when he coined a patriotic slogan: "ILA" he said, "means 'I Love America.'" This phrase was a popular one with longshoremen, and a union officer who used it as the climax of a speech could always be sure of an ovation.

Welfare Pension Committee, 1951. Standing: E.V. Watts, administrator, Jefferson Davis, Carlyle Barton, Joseph Laun, J.J. Brune, J.H. Threadgill, H. Franklin Sheely, August Idzik.

Author's Collection

August Idzik was about six feet tall, weighing over 200 pounds, a rugged and imposing individual. He was unusual in that he seldom, if ever, wore an overcoat, gloves or rubbers in cold and snowy weather. In his early years as a labor leader he was loud, argumentative, abrasive and determined in his speeches. Under Jefferson Davis's guidance he was quick to learn new tactics to gain his objectives. Mr. Idzik was a good student and although he was fiercely loyal to his men he learned to moderate his language and control his temper. He had an excellent memory, was smart and clever in negotiating and soon gained the respect of the maritime community.

In 1947, the term man-high, a much mentioned hyphenated word in the days before fork lifts, was emphasized when labor refused to pile bags of sugar in a warehouse higher than eight feet. At a committee meeting on the site it was agreed that shoulder height was man-high, a rule to be followed for all times. It was an example of what was to come as labor sought to limit slingloads and pallets loads, and objected to certain use of gear.

November 12, 1948 began a period of intermittent strikes which would extend into the Seventies. It brought the first intervention by government mediators when Cyrus Ching's formula for settlement was accepted by both parties sixteen days later. Of particular note was the inclusion of an item agreed to by management:

"A practical Welfare Plan, fair to both sides, is to be developed by a joint committee, to become effective on January 1, 1949. The entire cost of which is to be borne by the employers."

This plan was to be followed by another one of equal importance, the Pension Plan, started on December 20, 1950. The two plans have grown to multi-million dollar holdings and the administration with labor and management serving as joint trustees has become a model sought by other ports.

These were the days of free shape, and management's perogative to decide whether or not to continue in rain or other bad weather. Both were fought by labor. Some stevedore companies did take undue advantage of the free shape as they ordered their choice gangs on call, knowing that they would not have orders, simply to deny their use by competitors. These tactics were eliminated in a new contract signed in September, 1953. The rain clause was to be later challenged through arbitration which resulted in the Judge Niles decision of December 5, 1953 which determined that:

"Fresh gangs are entitled to 4 hours pay regardless of whether the employer or employee decides weather is too inclement to continue."

He also stated that men did not have to work on the pier, unloading box cars for example, during the guaranteed period. Due to this decision the men now refuse to work in slightly inclement weather. This has given the port a bad reputation.

Jefferson Davis died on October 1, 1953 and to this day he is recognized as the greatest representative the black race had in port labor circles. August Idzik became International Vice President of the ILA. William Haile, who in a quieter way was as effective as Davis, was appointed Atlantic Coast Vice President. He was a man of tact and patience—qualities not always found on the waterfront. Although Mr. Haile was usually a direct and businesslike speaker, he was also given to bits of poetic and sharply expressed philosophy. "A lie goes faster than truth. You have to be a truthful man to live down an untruth. You may tell an untruth to get a man to feel good, but

Loading sugar at American Sugar Refinery, 1935 *Enoch Pratt Free Library*

you will get defeated in the end. Humility in dealing with men costs you nothing. All men want praise and respect..."

Negotiations for the new contract opened in New York in the summer of 1956. A major demand of the ILA was a Master Contract to cover every port from Penobscot Bay, Maine, to Brownsville, Texas. Baltimore had been given assurance by the New York Shipping Association that it would never accede to a Master Contract. Little progress was accomplished during the next few months as the ILA struck on November 15. They were satisfied with the wage offer but still demanded an industry-wide contract. A federal court restraining order forced the men back for a 10-day period, later extended to the full 80 days in the Taft-Hartley Act. On February 12, 1957, at the end of the "cooling off period," labor again struck.

The Federal Mediation and Conciliation Panel suggested that management concede a Master Contract extending from Portland, Maine to Hampton Roads, Virginia. On February 18, 1957, the New York Shipping Association entered into a preliminary settlement with the ILA, incorporating the Master Contract. New York then sought to have the outports quickly accept the settlement. The Steamship Trade

Association, handling the local labor negotiations, was soon to experience the height of frustration. Having a definite understanding with the NYSA that it would never agree to a Master Contract, the S.T.A. met with labor delegates for many weeks conceding other demands. The deliberations did not come without pressure from New York interests. For three days Baltimore refused to accept and the pressure increased. Trade members were cautioned by their principals to give in or else. Agents and stevedores were threatened with changes in representation. At 10:30 PM on February 21, 1957, the Trade buckled under the pressure and finally had to concede not only the Master Contract, but all other concessions made during their meetings with labor.

In the late Fifties, the American Sugar Refinery changed its method of handling raw sugar. It had long been the practice to move this within burlap bags, which required the use of a large gang working a hatch, simultaneously with a similar size gang to discharge the product. A vessel might require a week, working around the clock, to handle a full cargo. In 1959, the company equipped its facility with two gantry cranes and began to receive cargoes in bulk. This made a drastic change in manpower needs. The gantries could work the cargo in rapid fashion with one-tenth the manpower. The changeover had already taken place in Philadelphia, and with the deep-sea locals involved, the ire of the ILA was aroused. The union demanded and received the first royalty payment when management agreed to deposit into a fund 25¢ per long ton which presumably was to compensate those who had been displaced by machines. Plans were to use the fund ultimately for the benefit of all because the men who worked sugar exclusively would be absorbed within the ranks of general cargo handlers and so dilute their earnings. A class action suit was brought against this disposition by a number of longshoremen who worked the sugar dock. Litigation ensued, and it was some time before the monies were finally deposited into the STA-ILA Pension Fund, at the mutual agreement of management and labor.

Negotiations for a new contract to begin October 1, 1959 were opened on August 10. Having been burned severely in the recent past, Baltimore simply awaited developments in New York. The ILA sought a 50% increase in wages and 100% in fringe benefits. Restrictive working conditions were to be introduced. Most important of all was a request for royalty payments on cargo handled by automated means. The result of these demands was another strike on October 1. On application of the National Labor Relations Board, a Federal district court issued a temporary order on October 8, restraining the union from striking. On December 10, the ILA and the NYSA agreed on a three-year contract covering the North Atlantic Ports which provided a 46¢ per hour package over the contract period. On the issue of container-ization, the parties agreed to retain th standard gang size, to use ILA members when containers were loaded or unloaded at the pier, and to further discuss the question of penalty payments for containers loaded or unloaded off the ship.

It was agreed that the question of these penalty payments would be submitted to arbitration if the parties could not settle the problem. After months of deliberation the matter was submitted to a board of arbitration. The "Stein Award" issued on November 16, 1960 was an extensive document requiring management to contribute a certain sum for tons of cargo loaded or unloaded by means of container use. August Idzik, then International Vice President of the ILA, representing Baltimore, suggested that the monies be deposited in the Pension Fund. Everyone distinctly recalls his expression that, "somewhere, somehow, sometime, some son of a ......will try to get his hands on the funds" and therefore insisted that they be placed in the Pension Fund for safekeeping. A beautiful expression at that time and typical of his desire always to protect Baltimore's interests.

When he died in 1962 the port lost one of its strongest advocates. William Haile succeeded him as the new international vice president of the ILA and John Kopp was appointed Atlantic Coast Vice President.

With the expiration of the stevedoring contract in September 1962, and anticipating difficulties brought about by automation, management and labor met in New York on June 13, 1962. The ILA demands consisted of six legal sheets. Automation was beginning to take its toll in the loss of man hours and the demands reflected this concern.

The Shipping Association responded on July 1, 1962, by submitting counter-proposals, the preamble of which read "We already advised at our last meeting that your proposals for a new contract are so unreasonable and costly that they cannot serve as a basis for realistic bargaining." The Association then went into detail revealing the need for increases in productivity, emphasizing, "The latest available official government data, for the ten year period from 1950 to 1960 show that average hourly longshore earnings increased 53.7% while cargo tonnage handled per manhour, during the same period, went down by 14.1%. This is in sharp contrast to the national productivity in other industries during the same period which went up 31%. The resultant gain in longshore wages and fringe benefits accompanied by the decrease in productivity, has boosted cargo handling labor costs by 100%. For our industry to keep pace with the national trend in increased productivity while at the same time preserving increased earnings of waterfront workers it is proposed that we jointly re-evaluate present work practices of more than a half-a-century which have become outdated by new developments in the steamship industry."

Unable to reach a settlement, labor struck on October 1. The Taft-Hartley Act was again invoked and labor was forced to return to work. This, incidentally, was the fifth time since 1948 that longshoremen had been ordered back to work through court action. The injunction expired on Christmas Eve, 1962 and the men again struck. Agreement was finally reached on January 25 with a wage increase of 24¢ per manhour over two years and a 9¢ per hour increase contribution to the pension fund. A total of 39 days of idleness had come to an end, the longest strike up to that time.

Mr. Idzik's prophecy came true on February 1, 1964 when the New York *Times* printed an article, under the heading "COURT BARS UNION FROM PORT FUNDS" which read, "An attempt by the International Longshoremen's Association to collect a $75,000 slice of the port of Baltimore automation fund has been blocked by a U.S. Court of Appeals ruling that such a payment would violate the nation's labor laws."

In September, 1964 labor presented management with its usual demands. One—asking for a guaranteed annual income—was to cause management many headaches for years to come. New York, at the suggestion of a Federal mediator, guaranteed 1,600 hours. To compensate for this the general cargo gang was to be reduced by two. But it was so difficult to implement this that it was agreed to forego its introduction until April 1, 1966.

In Baltimore the Steamship Trade Association had difficulty trying to persuade labor to dispense with the guarantee. It was finally able to convince some delegates that implementing it could result in a large loss of work to New York. The expense involved would be enormous. Would it not be better to await the experience in New York, the Association asked, before risking a detrimental loss of man-hours in Baltimore? The majority of labor leaders accepted this reasoning although there was to be no change in the gang structure.

The men on the docks resented the failure to obtain a guaranteed wage and voted on January 27, 1965 to reject the contract. Teddy Gleason, president of the ILA, was upset over the rejection. He had a contract in New York and he could not order his men back to work on the tradition of one port down, all ports down. John Bowers was sent to Baltimore to speak to the delegates and persuaded them to hold a new vote. This occurred on February 1, 1965 and the men accepted. However, there were many dissenters on the docks, led by the head of local 829, and the men refused to work. The leader was threatened with dismissal and revocation of the local's charter by Mr. Gleason, but to no avail. It required a court restraining order to force the men to work on February 13. Thus ended another lengthy strike period of 32 days. The contract was to extend for four years, terminating in September, 1968.

The difficulties with labor persisted, and Baltimore was to have an unusual disturbance. The leader of local 829, dissatisfied by the lack of a guarantee, called the men out on strike on January 26, 1966. Presumably it was because of a dispute over the number of men to be used in a gang when loading pig iron but it was obvious that the real reason was a dispute within the ILA itself. The head of Local 829 was unhappy with the leadership of that Association, and the wildcat strike was called more as a show of strength on his part. Then men of local 858 honored the contract and continued to work. It was only through another court order that the strike ended on February 7, 1966.

Other developments magnified the problems. Land-bridge and Mini-bridge were new terms. Again these designs would work against the dockworker and stevedore. Land-bridge, for instance, were cargoes originating in the Far East and moving in containers to West coast docks, there to be loaded on railroad flat cars to be hauled to the eastern seaboard, then to be loaded intact for European destinations. Traffic which formerly originated in the Far East for transit through the Panama Canal then to be unloaded by ILA labor, was being replaced by the new system. Mini-bridge was worse. This traffic offloads from container vessels on the West coast and moves to eastern destinations by rail, there to be sent to the consignee's door or to the distributors. The same systems work in reverse. The stevedore and dockworker were seeing work availability diminish.

On July 10, 1968, the first meeting on the new stevedore wage contract was held in New York. Teddy Gleason argued that he would not permit management to guarantee an annual income only for New York, and accused the New York Shipping Association, in consort with Liner services, of trying to concentrate work in New York.

The many meetings between management and labor brought few constructive results. Once again labor struck on October 1, and again the government intervened by obtaining a restraining order. The usual extension in the full 80 days was later obtained, which meant undisturbed work until December 20, 1968.

Prior to the termination of the Taft-Hartley injunction on December 20, the New York Shipping Association submitted a proposal which, in addition to generous monetary awards, also agreed to a 2,080 hour guarantee. Labor rejected the proposal and the entire coast struck. The offer was little different from that which was finally accepted. The real problem was not New York, but the outports, particularly Baltimore. None wanted to concede an extensive guaranteed wage.

After many meetings, the Steamship Trade, with the approval of the membership, finally conceded a guaranteed wage for 1800 hours. To implement this the Trade Association had to establish a Central Dispatching Office. The ILA agreed to reduce the general cargo gang by three men. The men returned to work on February 20, 1969, having been idle for the longest period in history, 62 days.

In February, 1971, management and labor were shocked by a federal court order which declared that within a period of 90 days from February 19, the ILA, in conjunction with the Atlantic Coast District, shall revoke the existing charters of locals 829 and 858 in Baltimore and issue a single charter with a new charter number. The order also included a stipulation that a port seniority plan be adopted. A stevedore company could no longer assign its good gangs to certain jobs. Every gang had to have an equal opportunity for employment. With a stroke of his pen, Judge Alexander Harvey upset hiring practices that had been in use for decades. The productivity of the port was immediately and drastically reduced and has continued downward to the present day.

During this time the ILA seemed to think of itself as an element of the Department of State. Whenever something happened in a foreign country not to its liking, the ILA refused to handle cargo to and from that country. Even today most Russian exports (e.g. nickle and cotton linters) consigned to the United States are being unloaded in Canadian ports and shipped in rail cars or trucks to destinations in the States. The port has lost considerable tonnage in the last eleven years due to this decision. A recent Supreme Court ruling has made this position unconstitutional.

In early June, 1971, the ILA met with management on the contract to supplant the one expiring in September. The ILA asked double time for overtime and sixteen paid holidays. Despite an early start in the negotiations the result was the same— another strike—another Taft-Hartley injunction. After a 48-day strike the ILA and the Steamship Trade Assocation agreed to a three year contract which included an 1,900 hour guaranteed wage, 77¢ per hour increase in benefits and $1.50 per hour increase in wages spread over the three years.

The port lost an outstanding labor leader when William Haile died in 1973, a man who took pardonable pride in the men of the port. John Kopp became international vice president of the ILA and Hersey Richardson was appointed Atlantic Coast vice-president.

On March 26, 1974, the ILA through its president Teddy Gleason announced that it would open up joint negotiating sessions with management representatives the next day. Mr. Gleason, chief negotiator for labor, said "that these early bargaining sessions established a 'first' for meeting with management and he was optimistic that all issues and demands could be established early, enabling both sides to get on with negotiating a contract long before the expiration date of September 30, 1974." He further stated that "it was his hope that a contract could be negotiated without a strike, and it was his strategy that early meetings could possibly achieve this." The initial proposal submitted to management called for a one year contract and with unrealistic demands.

Mr. Gleason was beginning to realize that the actions in the past, although most productive to his membership, were beginning to take their toll on the availability of work in his own New York area. Strategy certainly dictated that it was in his best interest to bargain for a prompt settlement. To do otherwise would continue to force the business to Canadian ports, which had prospered through the numerous strikes in the states.

A new contract was signed on June 21, 1974, the first completed without a work stoppage in nearly 30 years. The agreement called for an 82¢ per hour increase in benefits and $1.90 per hour increase in wages spread over three years.

The Baltimore shipping interests were relieved that there would not be a strike. This prompted many news articles, such as this appearing in the *Intermodal World:*

"An agreement at such an early date appears to be proof of a newly found maturity on all sides. The lessons of the past damaging work stoppages finally seem to have been learned by all involved. For once, the regular flow of trade will—hopefully—not be interrupted and there will be no losses to individual business as well as to the nation's overall balance of payment, which was always among the first to be hurt by a longshore strike."

On June 8, 1977, almost four months prior to the termination of the contract, the ILA submitted its wage demands for a new contract, again with requests that staggered the Steamship Trade Association. A report published in New York reflecting the history of innovative change covering a period from 1951 to 1975 indicated that in 1951, 48,000 men worked a total of 46,000,000 manhours moving some 22,000,000 tons of general cargo. Twenty three years later, 14,000 worked 22,000,000 manhours to move 27,000,000 tons of general cargo. The expected adverse effect on the dockworker from containerization was clearly taking its toll.

The contract expired on September 30, and the ILA selectively struck only the automated carriers, allowing the conventional operators to continue. Finally in mid-November a new agreement was reached calling for 91¢ per hour increase in benefits and $2.40 per hour increase in wages spread over the three year contract.

In addition to a generous monetary settlement amounting to 30.5% over three years, the ILA was to finally break through on industry bargaining. A contract-outside-the-contract finally satisfied Mr. Gleason when a new concept was agreed upon to be known as "Job Security Program." It was to apply in every Atlantic and Gulf coast port and was a major concession on management's part. Its adoption was a milestone in the annals of ILA successes. While it does nothing to increase job preservation, it does assure that the funds will always be protected and the men can rest comfortably knowing that their future is secure.

The program was to be funded by assessing each weight ton of 2,240 lbs. moving in and out of every participating port, in this manner:

1—Containers & Automated Cargo . . . . 20¢ per ton
2—Break-bulk Cargo . . . . 12¢ per ton
3—Bulk Cargo . . . . 2¢ per ton

The all-coast ports entered into a three-year agreement with the ILA on the seven master contract issues on May 24, 1980. It was the earliest agreement ever reached in the history of negotiations. Baltimore concluded all local conditions in late August and signed the three-year contract on September 9. This era of peace was not to begin without the usual granting of increases to labor—$3.60 per hour in wages and $1.20 per hour in benefits spread over the three years.

It is interesting to note that the base wage rate for straight time will show a growth from 85¢ per hour in 1929 with no fringe benefits to that of $14.00 with fringes costing about $7.00 per hour, for a total of $21.00 on September 1, 1982. The effect of automation on the longshore industry is far from settled as there is always the possibility of disagreements between management and labor. The clause in the agreement which permits labor to terminate the contract on 60 days notice if any item within the contract is declared illegal, void, or unenforceable, makes for a constant threat.

On the subject of their work and achievements, the local longshoremen are anything but modest. "We're the pace-setters," exclaimed a young stevedore. "Baltimore longshoremen are the best in the business. We're second to nobody." Venerable Eugene Foster, who retired in 1960 after a half-century of longshoring, praised today's dock gangs with their improved equipment, but recalls a time when "Longshoremen were proud of their strength and were always anxious to lift any weight just to prove they could do it. Now longshoremen won't lift anything over 50 pounds by hand."

William Haile, the eminent labor leader, once described the container as the coffin of the longshoremen. Initially, it did create fear, but as this is being written, the benefits accruing to a large segment of men on the dock is such that rather than a coffin, it has produced countless advantages in earnings and job security. The longshoreman has advanced from a rough and tumble worker to one in the higher strata of working men, and his earnings are among the best in the industrial world.

Stevedoring before containerization, 1950's

Author's Collection

COAL—NEW GROWTH FOR THE PORT

FOR THE PAST 100 years coal has had an important role in the development of the port. It began in the late 1860's when John Garrett built the Locust Point terminal which included a small coal pier to bunker steamships.

In 1872 the Philadelphia, Wilmington & Baltimore Railroad built a coal pier at the foot of East Avenue, and six years later two Baltimore businessmen, Bernard N. Baker and James S. Whitely, erected a 400-foot coal pier in lower Canton. In 1879 the port had handled over 100,000 tons of coal.

An increased demand for modern facilities for bunkering and loading coal for Europe was made in the early 1900's. The Western Maryland Railway opened a new coal pier in Port Covington on September 24, 1904, backed by a holding yard capable of storing over 200 cars. The Pennsylvania Railroad purchased the antiquated Baker-

Holding yard for coal, Port Covington, 1904

Baltimore Street Car Museum

The Port—Pride of Baltimore / 129

Whitely coal pier on South Clinton Street to build a new pier 1100 feet long with a loading capacity of 900 tons per hour. It was completed in 1917. With that, the port became the East Coast's leading coaling station.

World War I resulted in a great demand for energy in war torn Europe and the B & O recognized the need for modern coal facilities. The railroad constructed a new coal pier, designed by the company's engineers, near Stonehouse Cove in Curtis Bay and completed in 1918. It was the first major bulk coal pier in this country utilizing high capacity belt conveyors and traveling ship loaders.

After fire destroyed the Western Maryland Railway's coal pier at Port Covington on September 5, 1919 it was replaced by a modern one. Opened on April 1, 1921 the pier was 888 feet long with a loading capacity of 3,500 tons per hour.

The Curtis Bay coal pier was upgraded in 1968 at a cost of $11,000,000 with the installation of single and double rotary car dumpers capable of handling 120-ton cars, one traveling electric barge loader and one traveling electric ship loader. A conveyor system with main belts 72" and 84" wide, blends sizes of coal. The pier is 900 feet long and 117 feet wide with a loading capacity of 6,000 tons per hour. When the B & O and the Western Maryland Railway merged in 1972 loading coal was concentrated at the more efficient Curtis Bay pier and the Port Covington pier was closed in 1974.

Selection of Baltimore by coal producers and carriers as the logical location for large investments in new coal export facilities is providing the port with its greatest potential for growth in recent years. In 1980, $145,000,000 of industrial revenue bonds were committed for new coal facilities, of which $90,000,000 has already been

Wooden bark Shenandoah loading coal, Locust Point, 1907

Peale Museum

Western Maryland Railway Coal pier, Port Covington, c 1960   *A. Aubrey Bodine*

invested. By 1985 the port will be able to export at least 36,000,000 tons annually. The magnitude of this growth can be seen by comparing it to the 5,900,000 tons of 1978. For each ton of coal exported it is estimated that $21 is fed into the area's economy.

Coal producers and carriers have chosen to invest in the port for obvious reasons. Huge reserves of coal are located in Southwest Pennsylvania, Western Maryland and Northern West Virginia. This region is served in large part by the Western Maryland and B & O railroads and Baltimore is the major terminal port for both. Therefore, large reserves of coal are, in a real sense, captive to the port. In addition to its geographic location, the port has prime locations for the development of coal facilities.

Baltimore currently has one modern operational coal pier and two smaller ones. The major pier is the B & O's Curtis Bay facility. In 1979 it loaded 9,100,000 tons, 12,500,000 tons in 1980, and 14,000,000 tons in 1981.

In addition to the Curtis Bay coal pier, the Western Maryland Railway uses the Port Covington ore pier to load ships with coal that comes to Port Covington by barge from the Curtis Bay coal pier.

Consolidated Rail owns the old coal pier on Clinton Street in the Canton area. Unlike modern coal piers which utilize conveyor belts to carry coal from the cars to the ship, the old Conrail pier utilizes sixty 4-ton cars on a continuous cable. Conrail is now loading barges that are shifted to Rukert Terminals Pier 5 where the coal is loaded onto vessels with a floating crane. While the Port Covington and Canton operations cost more per ton of coal, they are still economically feasible because of the long, costly wait to use the regular facility at Curtis Bay. The makeshift systems allow the loading of from seven to nine additional ships per month—2,000,000 tons of coal per year.

Two coal producers have made large investments for new coal loading facilities, one at Curtis Bay, the other at Canton.

Kentucky-Ohio Transportation is building the Curtis Bay pier to load coal for the Island Creek Coal Company. Both are subsidiaries of Occidental Petroleum. Curtis Bay Company, a new subsidiary, will operate the facility which will be known as Bayside Terminals.

The first phase, the storage area for 500,000 tons, was finished in February, 1982, at a cost of about $30,000,000. It is behind and adjacent to the B & O Curtis Bay Coal pier. Coal stored here can be loaded from either the B & O pier or the new Occidental pier next to the B & O pier. Completion of the new $30,000,000 pier is expected in the first quarter of 1983. It will have an annual loading capacity of 12,000,000 tons annually.

Artist's rendering of Canton facilities of Consolidation Coal Company, scheduled for opening in 1983
Consolidation Coal Co.

In September, 1980 Consolidation Coal Company purchased from the Canton Company 110 acres of waterfront property, the Cottman ore pier and the Canton Railroad which consists of 39 miles of track for $30,000,000.

The storage area will have an on-the-ground storage capacity of 750,000 tons and will be able to accommodate 100,000 car arrivals annually. Consolidation will extensively redevelop and transform the Cottman ore pier into a coal-loading one to load ships on one side, barges on the other. Initially, it will load 10,000,000 tons and service 175 to 200 ships annually. The coal will come from Pennsylania, West Virginia, Western Maryland and possibly Kentucky.

Consolidation Coal has made an irreversible commitment of $110,000,000. Seventy million is to cover the cost of equipment and construction of a storage facility and coal pier, $30,000,000 the purchase of Canton Company assets and $10,000,000 for unexpected costs. The target date for completion is the first quarter of 1983.

Dramatic increases in export coal shipments has obvious impacts upon the proposed 50-foot channel.

THE YEARS AHEAD

DURING MY 50 years on the Baltimore waterfront it has been my privilege to see the port grow from primarily a steel and bulk port to one of the finest general cargo ports on the East Coast.

I have watched the greatest change in the methods of handling cargo in the history of stevedoring: Once it was back-breaking work handling each individual package with hooks and hand trucks. Now we have lift trucks handling pallets of two tons each and cranes capable of lifting containers with 20 tons of general cargo. Handling of bulk materials has changed from work with picks, shovels, and iron tubs to conveyors and high speed cranes, equipped with grab buckets, discharging 600–800 tons per hour.

Diking of Canton Seagirt Marine Terminal, 1982   *Maryland Port Administration*

Artist's conception, completed Canton Seagirt Marine Terminal. When completed in the late 1980's will have estimated capacity of 2,225,000 tons annually
Maryland Port Administration

Masonville, Southwest Branch of the Patapsco River
Maryland Port Administration

Artist's conception, 350-acre marine terminal, Masonville when completed in 1990's.

Maryland Port Administration

I would be remiss not to mention some of the outstanding men whom I was fortunate to meet during part of my career—like Jefferson Davis and August Idzik who were 100 percent union but fair when dealing with the employers. Also such business executives as Robert Fleagle, Steve Masson, Joseph Brune, Arch Seidel, and many other fine individuals, too numerous to mention, who spent hours attending important port committee meetings and contributing much to the enhancement of the port.

The visit of the tall ships to Baltimore in July, 1976, celebrating our nation's 200th birthday, created a feeling of excitement and enthusiasm throughout the state. Hundreds of thousands of Marylanders visited the port for the first time and left deeply impressed not only with the tall ships but with the modern port facilities. Operation Sail 1976 had a predominant role in educating both Baltimoreans and Marylanders to the vital economic value the port of Baltimore has for the entire state.

Baltimore has been rewarded over the years for its early confidence in the container concept, and portwide the growth in container cargo has been impressive. The amount of container tonnage moving through the port in 1981, about 4,400,000 tons, was almost 50 times greater than the 89,000 tons of 1965, one of the first years container figures were recorded.

In short, Baltimore has impressive container facilities already available, and plans for the future include the construction of the Sea-Girt Marine Terminal scheduled to be operational within the decade. Long range plans call for the construction of another terminal at Masonville. With the port's container traffic approaching 5,000,000 tons annually, Baltimore is confident of becoming the number one container port in the United States. Based on past performance, it is certainly a realistic and attainable goal.

The two new coal facilities under construction will provide an incremental annual increase of up to 35,000,000 short tons in the port's export capacity. They will generate over 5,500 jobs for Maryland residents and nearly $240,000,000 of income.

In addition to the future employment, income, personal income and sales tax, and revenue impacts, these two new facilities will stimulate economic activity in the state.

The continued development of the port remains vital to the economic well-being of Maryland. The dredging and deepening of the channel becomes even more urgent because of the burgeoning world-wide demand for coal. It is imperative that this long-delayed project get underway as soon as possible.

The diking of the Hart/Miller Islands will protect the Chesapeake Bay's ecosystem. When finished it will become a permanent 1,140 acre wildlife and public recreational area.

In addition to the continuing need for a 50-foot channel there is equal need for the development of dredged spoil disposal sites for project and maintenance dredging spoil. Today the private sector must pay about $10 per cubic yard for dredging work in the port if they are lucky enough to find a place to dispose of this spoil. Comparable figures for such work in Norfolk is closer to $2 per cubic yard.

I am optimistic about the future of the port or we at Rukert's would not be spending $2,500,000 to erect a high-speed bulk unloading crane. I feel the State of Maryland has been remiss in encouraging private investment and development in the port. Port projects are generally of such a highly capital intensive nature that they pose significant financing and amortization problems. Interest rates in the private sector compared to those in the public sector bond market gives one clear indication of the comparative difficulty facing the private investor.

The State should carry out its mandate "to improve the facilities and strengthen the workings of the private port operator."

"The Port of Baltimore can be correctly described as Maryland's greatest asset."

This is the finding of what is probably the most comprehensive survey ever made of a major United States port, fully confirming what members of Maryland's maritime community have long suspected.

The survey, "The Economic Impact of the Port of Baltimore of Maryland," was prepared by Drs. Stanley J. Hille and James E. Suelflow, of the College of Business and Public Administration of the University of Maryland.

The year surveyed was 1966, the first offering adequate statistics after the initiation of the study. During the year the port handled some 21,933,500 tons of cargo valued at $2,220,000.

It showed that the industrial, commercial and transportation complex making up the port annually pours some $626,900,000 in Maryland's economy while directly providing jobs for 62,138 Marylanders. This is the primary impact. It generates, in turn, a secondary impact estimated at no less than $1,560,000,000, representing 11.7% of the gross State product.

"The Port of Baltimore represents Maryland's largest industry and its most valuable asset," was the conclusion of an impact study of the port's business based on 1980 statistics.

The study reported that nearly 79,000 Maryland residents were employed by organizations related to the port. An additional 30,000 secondary jobs were created as a result of port trade and commerce.

The study was made by Booz, Allen & Hamilton, Inc., an internationally known consultant firm. It calculated that some 24,000 jobs were directly generated by the port, and that these workers had incomes totaling $529,000,000. In addition, the study showed that $52,000,000 in state and local taxes were generated by the port.

Containerized cargo generated 37 percent of the total port revenue in 1980. Coal and grain accounted for about 40 percent of the total tonnage.

Pier 5 Bulk Unloading Crane

The study, "The Economic Impact of the Port of Baltimore," was commissioned by the Greater Baltimore Committee in conjunction with the Maryland Port Administration, the Steamship Trade Assocation of Baltimore, the Maryland Chamber of Commerce and the Maryland Pilots Association.

Foreign waterborne commerce in the port during 1981 amounted to 35,200,000 tons. This represents a 4.4 percent portwide decline in the flow of cargo from the prior year, or 1,600,000 tons less than 1980. Baltimore showed its strength as a competitive East Coast port in limiting cargo losses during a period of international recession and severe attacks on its markets by Canadian and West Coast diversions.

According to the 1980 survey, if all port activities were to cease, it is estimated the $1,200,000,000 of economic activity would have to be regained in some other way to replace the port loss.

Dr. John Stevenson's prophetic vision 130 years earlier of Baltimore town as an ever-growing world port, her economy resting on coast-wise and overseas commerce and industry, is now more than ever an established fact.

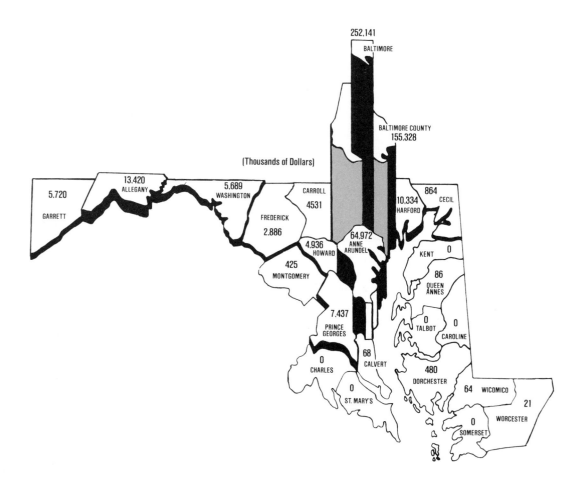

Geographic Distribution of Income Impact excluding respending (Thousands of Dollars)
Booz, Allen & Hamilton Report (1982)

PURELY PERSONAL—AN EPILOGUE

I WILL NEVER FORGET the first time my father, W. G. Norman Rukert, later known as "Cap," took me down to the Baltimore harbor. It was a hot Saturday in July when he asked me if I would like to see a German vessel being discharged with bulk potash. In those days I seldom saw my father as he worked seven days a week—usually long days—and I was often asleep when he came home.

As we walked into the Block Street Wharf warehouse the dust was so thick you could cut it with a knife. The men shoveling potash were stripped to the waist and so wet with perspiration it looked like someone had dipped them overboard. I was scared to death as we climbed the shaky ladder to board the vessel. As we moved along the deck I was amazed at its size and length. The men were shoveling potash into large iron tubs which were then hoisted out of the hatch and dumped into a hopper. My father introduced me to the captain who took us up to the bridge and showed me how to read the compass and let me turn the ship's wheel. From the bridge I looked over the side and saw men pulling two-wheeled carts (Georgia buggies) filled with potash. I thought mules should be pulling them instead of men. Little did I realize that some years later I would be pulling the same carts.

When I got home that afternoon, I felt that I had returned from a different world, but it was a day that I will never forget.

Fifteen years later I began to understand why I saw little of my father during my early childhood.

He started to work at the age of 14 as a cub reporter for the Baltimore *American,* the oldest paper in the city. He helped cover the great Baltimore fire of February, 1904 which swept away the newspaper's office and about 1,500 other downtown buildings. The fire did not eliminate his job, but one of his later assignments ended his newspaper career. One day his father heard that his son had been assigned to cover the city's red light district and immediately he found a new job for him as a clerk at the Jackson's Wharf station of the Pennsylvania Railroad. After a few years he became a stock clerk with the Terminal Warehouse Company.

Years followed, and while at the Terminal, at the start of World War I, he was commissioned a captain and assigned to the Colgate warehouse at Camp Holabird. Immediately after the war he was appointed warehouse superintendent at the Block Street Wharf and Warehouse Company in Fells Point. By 1921, with his experience in warehousing, he was convinced that he could go into business for himself. The most important reason for the success of the new venture was an $800 unsecured loan given him by Heyward Boyce of the Drovers & Mechanics Bank.

A few days after securing the loan, maritime circles were buzzing with the news that French shippers were planning to resume sending potash to the United

States after a long war-time interruption. He knew that potash had once been stored at the Block Street Wharf property before the war, so he approached the Chesapeake Bank, which owned the complex, and arranged a ten-year lease. My father was able to convince the French shipping interests that he had a facility available that could handle the vessel which was on its way to Baltimore. They agreed to a long-term contract that proved so successful that later the German potash industry entered into a similar agreement.

As the waterfront business became more profitable, my father decided to look for more business space. In 1927, he was advised that Jackson's Wharf, at Caroline and Thames Streets, owned by McCormick & Company, was available for $135,000. He only had $3,000 for a down payment, but Willoughby McCormick, founder of the international tea and spice firm, was convinced of his sincerity and ability. He told him to go ahead, and pay off the price out of profits.

Three years later, the Southern Pacific S/S Lines, of New York, began organizing weekly sailing to Galveston and Houston and was looking for a new terminal in Baltimore. After inspecting the new Jackson's Wharf facility, it entered into an agreement with Rukert to handle stevedoring, receiving and delivery of their weekly cargoes.

Colgate Warehouse, Camp Holabird   *Author's Collection*

On June 1, 1931 I came to work for my father at Rukert Terminals as a laborer on the pier loading and unloading trucks of freight for the Southern Pacific. I had just graduated from City College two weeks before my sixteenth birthday and I was more interested in going to college or starting a career in baseball. Even the diversionary tactic of my father sending me on a trip to Galveston and Houston on the *S/S El Estero,* a Southern Pacific freighter, did not change my dreams of baseball or college. But that was not to be. During the next two years I held the company's record, and perhaps Baltimore harbor's also, for being fired. But I had a secret angel; every time my father would send me home, my mother would immediately send me

W.G. Norman "Cap" Rukert
Author's Collection

back to work. I did learn a valuable lesson then—it was much easier riding back and forth on a streetcar then working as a laborer on the docks.

This was the toughest time of my life—working from sunup to sundown—7 days a week, then going to bed as soon as I got home, too tired to eat. It seemed to me that the boss's son was always given the hardest job, such as loading carbon black in bags. At the time I thought I had been given this job because in a short time I would be the same color as the rest of the gang. It was a red letter day in my life when my father advanced money (which was never repaid) to the International Longshoremen to organize a warehouse local which meant an 8-hour day for me. But years later during our wage negotiations with the same union I regretted that my father had been so generous.

Despite the hard work I had a number of experiences, some humorous, and some not too humorous, which I will never forget. I always worked under my father's four black foremen, George Northern, John Grimes, Henry Hughes and John Chase. Only being the boss's son often saved me from bodily harm.

George Northern was a short, well-built man with huge hands. One day I was told that George could pick up 15 billiard balls, 8 in the right hand and 7 with the left. I refused to believe it so I bet him $1, one-tenth of my weekly salary. During a lunch hour we slipped away to a billiard parlor and within a few minutes I knew I would be without Coke money for the rest of the week.

John Grimes, a tall, muscular man, stuttered when he was excited. He was a sight to see, spitting and stammering, when my father gave him hell for something. I will never forget the day he and another man were loading bags of flour on a truck and I was given a needle and twine to recooper any damaged bags. Everything went smoothly until I saw John bending over with his back toward me. The target became so tempting, that I stuck the needle in his backside. He leaped up screaming, and made a grab for me. Unfortunately he missed. I dropped the needle and ran down the pier and hid until he had quieted down.

Henry Hughes, a tall, lanky man was my favorite pigeon. Henry had a great fear of rats—and the pier was loaded with them. One day while recoopering flour I found a nest of six hairless baby rats. I knew Hughes kept his lunch in a brown paper bag in the boiler room where the men ate their lunch. I put the rats in a similar bag, took it to the boiler room and substituted it for his lunch bag. At noon Henry picked up his lunch, sat down at the table and proceeded to tear open the bag. As the six baby rats jumped out he leaped up, turned ten shades lighter and dashed out of the door. The last time I saw him that day he was running up Caroline Street.

I never felt comfortable working with John Chase. No job was too difficult for him, and he could drive the men in his gang better than anyone I have ever known. One hot summer night Chase had a gang of eight shoveling bulk potash, which was being unloaded from a vessel into one of our warehouses. At 11 PM five of the men knocked off, exhausted from the extreme heat and humidity. I knew that the vessel would continue to work regardless, but unless we kept the potash pile up we would not be able to take the cargo. I asked Chase what we should do and he told me to get my car and he and I would find replacements. We went to a bar at Caroline and Bond Streets which was packed and jammed. As we entered the bar he called out in his booming voice, "I want five men to work the rest of the night." No one stirred, so he went up and down the bar and picked out five men, all in some form of intoxication and told them if they did not go quietly he would carry them out bodily. And he could. He was a big man $6\frac{1}{2}$ feet tall, weighed 250 pounds and was all muscle. We crammed them into my Model A Ford, and got back to the warehouse at midnight. About 3

A.M. the liquor began to wear off and the men began to wonder what they were doing. One became belligerent and picked a fight with Chase, who nonchalantly picked up a shovel and hit him so hard it knocked him unconscious. As he fell his head hit the concrete wall opening a deep gash. John picked him up, put him in the front seat of my car and told me to take him to the hospital. I spent the balance of the night in St. Joseph's Hospital accident room on Caroline Street, but I can assure you that Chase did not have any trouble with the others for the balance of the night.

On a cold February day while I was weighing potash as it was being discharged from a vessel at the Block Street Wharf I witnessed a courageous act. One of the longshoremen in Will Smith's gang slipped overboard between the dock and the vessel. Without hesitating, Will Smith dove into the water and wedged himself between the vessel and one of the pilings and kept the vessel off the dock until both were pulled from the water. Will Smith, a slender, black man, would have been crushed to death had a gust of wind hit the vessel on the opposite side.

A month later at Jackson's Wharf Terminal one of our laborers, Henry Jones, was pulling a four-wheel wagon loaded with bags of flour up the pier when the right front wheel hit a piece of wood which jerked the tong and flipped Henry overboard. My father, who could not swim a stroke, jumped into the water and grabbed Henry and held onto a piling until we pulled them out of the cold water.

During the summer Henry was helping me unload new Chrysler automobiles out of box cars which were being loaded on the *El Estero* bound for Houston, Texas. As we took the cars out of the boxcar a licensed driver would move them to shipside. About 10:30 that morning I missed Henry and went looking for him. As I moved out to the pier I heard someone yell that a car had been driven overboard and I knew immediately it had to be Henry. Hours later when a crane lifted the car out of 27 feet of water Henry was still clutching the steering wheel. No one will ever know what possessed him to try and drive that car.

During a seamen's strike, in the middle of the 1930's, I was working a gang of men in Canton when I received a call from my father. He told me to bring four men to the Caroline Street Terminal to help shift the *S/S El Estero* to Sparrows Point. I knew the ship was scheduled to sail for Galveston, Texas that night, so I asked him if the schedule had been changed. "No," he replied, "the crew is four men short and the Coast Guard has refused to let the ship leave." He paused and then with emphasis continued, "Be sure to tell them that they are only going to Sparrows Point." I picked four of the youngest men, piled them into my car and drove them through the picket line and placed them aboard. Two hours later the vessel sailed for Galveston. That was the last time I ever saw them, I thought.

One winter night in 1963 my wife and I attended a dance at a local country club. While I was checking my coat, I was greeted with, "Hello, Cap, it's been over 30 years since I have seen you." I was speechless when I recognized the man behind the counter as one of the four I had shanghaied years before. But the tension was quickly broken when he said, "I want to thank you for putting me aboard the *S/S El Estero* that day. When I landed in Texas I was immediately hired as an able seaman on a tanker. After working at sea for 25 years for the same company. I retired with a fine pension." A happy ending for one, but I would certainly like to know what ever happened to the other three men.

In 1937, Rukert Terminals acquired Pier 5 at 2100 South Clinton Street in Canton and my father farmed me out to handle operations there. When he had occasion to call me, the office employees wondered why he used the phone. They used to say that all he had to do was to open his window. It faced the Canton area across the harbor and jokesters said his son could hear every word his father said without any help from the telephone system.

It was during this period I met two of my favorite characters—John Williams and J. Selby.

John Williams was born at 2113 South Clinton Street, next door to the tavern he later ran. His father was a sea captain in the Brazilian coffee trade and his mother an Army nurse during the Civil War. They married after the war and moved to Canton. On the wall of his tavern John Williams hung an illuminated certificate listing the 29 Civil War battles his father had been in. Behind the bar he kept his father's Civil War pistol, a meerschaum pipe that William Geyhouser, overseer at the Stickney blast furnace, had won from his boss, George Stickney, in an election bet about Lincoln.

While at Pier 5 I went to his tavern for a soda every lunch hour just to hear his stories. One was about his seafaring grandfather who disappeared during the California Gold Rush. Another was about an old soldier friend of his parents who struck oil in Texas after the Civil War, came back to Baltimore after Mr. Williams' mother died, and promised him "the prettiest monument in town" if he would open her grave and let him see her face once more. John declined.

He showed me how, as a child, he had made fishing tackle from drift sugar canes and bent pins to catch perch and spot off Clinton Street piers near his house.

John Williams had always owned racehorses, and he kept two trotters in the stable behind his tavern. Every time he would take me to see the horses he'd brag that one of them, a beautiful animal named Indian Maid, had a mark of 2:08. This remark made no sense to me then, but I have since learned that he was referring to the horse's track record in a mile race. Indian Maid had been a rather remarkable trotter.

In 1901 Mr. Williams laid out a small park on a piece of land across the street from his tavern. Covering not more than half an acre, the park was on a bluff overlooking the harbor and commanded a fine view of Fort McHenry. He planted flower beds and a hedge along the curb and found some discarded chairs and a bench. The area had no official name but from the remarks of curious passersby it came to be known as "I Wonder Park." Patterson Park, three miles to the north, was the nearest of its kind, so "I Wonder" was used by the children of Canton. And it was popular with stevedores and factory workers on their lunch break who played quoits and pitched horseshoes.

Mr. Williams had a herd of goats and he used them to keep the grass cropped and weeds down. He was forced to sell the goats after their leader, Billie, butted a Pennsylvania Railroad detective.

The park had six mulberry trees donated by a friend of his called Charles-Got-Your-Shoes-On-Wrong. Mr. Charles came from an area where the people used to change their shoes from one foot to the other to keep them straight. The children who played in the park gave him his name because one day he would wear his right shoe on the right foot, and the next day it would be on his left.

Because the park was located in such an unlikely spot among the wharves and fertilizer factories of Canton, it was a thrill to people driving down South Clinton Street to come across the flowers, the hedge, and the one lonely but inviting bench. In 1941 the Pennsylvania Railroad, owner of the property, leased it to the Maritime Commission which built an office and warehouse on the park grounds. A few years later Ripley's nationally-syndicated "Believe It or Not" feature portrayed "I Wonder Park" as the smallest in the world.

Today the only thing left to identify the location of this unusual park is a lone mulberry tree in front of the building at 2100 South Clinton Street.

A scow is a large, freight-carrying, flat-bottomed, square-ended boat towed by a tug. Atlantic Transport Company, founded in 1883, was one of the principal firms engaged in supplying scows for the movement of freight from ships to piers. Each scow had a man to catch the lines, count the cargo and sweep the floor after each shipment. Most Atlantic Transport scowmen were illiterate blacks, with a language and lifestyle of their own. Because the company was paid on the tonnage hauled, the scowmen used this method to calculate the amount of goods they were carrying: they

Esther Phillips

Author's Collection

would have someone determine how many coffee bags, canned goods or bags of fertilizer would fill a specified space and so mark the floor boards. When the scow was loaded, the scowman would make sure the goods reached that mark. In this way, even though he may have been ignorant of arithmetic, he made sure neither he nor his company was cheated.

J. Selby, a scowman for Atlantic Transport in the early 1900's, was a man with unusual talents. Though he had a peg leg, he could climb a rope ladder as well as any man. And he could paint. Tugboat captains logged their tugs' activities on pads of paper backed with cardboard. Selby would ask around for the cardboard, paint maritime scenes on it, and then try to sell the watercolors. One of his four works still known to exist is the *Esther Phillips,* an Atlantic Transport tug, with the Canton grain elevator in the background.

Years ago, before he retired as general manager of Atlantic Transport, Robert Fleagle bought this painting from a company dispatcher for $5 and put it in a desk drawer. He didn't particularly like the watercolor at the time, he says, but everytime he opened the drawer he saw it, so he had it framed at Bendann Art Galleries.

Mr. Fleagle says the proportions of the tug are not only exact, but the color of the *Esther Phillips* stacks was skillfully reproduced.

Abraham Rydberg

Author's Collection

Herbert L. Rawding
Mariners Museum, Newport News, Va.

The stacks were painted a Tuscan red, a pinkish-red color mixed for the company by a London firm. The only missing detail is the lack of highlights on the flag pole. He believes that Selby didn't want the lights to detract from the American flag so he left them out.

Captain Thomas J. Murphy, Jr., president of the Baker-Whitely Towing Company, has a beautiful watercolor by Selby of the three-masted schooner *Robert Fry*. The only other two known Selby watercolors, both of ships belonging to the Baltimore-Carolina Lines, are in the Maritime Museum of the Maryland Historical Society.

During my early career I loaded hundreds of Chesapeake Bay schooners and rams with freight for the Eastern Shore of Maryland but the two most interesting ventures were the unloading of the full-rigged sailing vessel *Abraham Rydberg* and the loading of the schooner *Herbert L. Rawding.*

The *Abraham Rydberg,* a Swedish training vessel, was the last full-rigged sailing ship to unload cargo in the port. On December 6, 1941, the day before Pearl Harbor, she sailed from Santos, Brazil, for Boston, with a cargo consisting of 68,200 bags of fertilizer of cottonseed meal with 5 per cent castor pomace added. The total weight was 3,410 tons. After battling bad weather and unfavorable winds for three months and with increased activity of German submarines, Oscar Malmber, the 30-year old captain, decided to bring the vessel to Baltimore instead of Boston. This was possible under the war risk clause of the bill of lading.

The Clipper ship, with her towering spars, was an inspiration to see as she passed Fort McHenry moving into the inner harbor. She docked at the foot of Caroline Street on March 15, 1942 to discharge her cargo. The vessel had no winches, but had a donkey boiler used to raise her anchor and hoist the sails. A swinging boom was rigged with rope falls, and with the help of the donkey boiler, the stevedores were able to discharge the cargo. This was a long and tedious job, as the bags beyond the hatch opening had to be brought by hand trucks to the square of the hatch. They were then loaded in eight-bag slings and lifted by the swinging boom to the dock. The cargo was discharged on March 31, 1942. While the vessel was unloaded, the ship officers held daily classes for the 42 cadets. The mornings were spent repairing sails and renewing ropes, then the decks were swabbed until they glistened. After lunch, instructions were given on navigation, compass and use of the sextant. The cadets, between 16 and 20 years old, sailed the ship themselves with the help of the captain, the mates, the boatswain, the sailmaker and the carpenter. Each had paid $200 for tuition and also supplied his own bedding. They spent a year aboard the Clipper, learning seamanship, navigation and more importantly, learning to depend on themselves and experience the value of unity, character-developing traits.

On April 1, 1942, the *Abraham Rydberg* was moved to anchorage, where she stayed until January, 1943, when she was purchased by Julio Riberio Campos of Portugal for a reported $265,000 and renamed *Fox de Douro*. A survey had shown that her steel hull was sound. Outfitting her for sea, however, presented a problem. Manila rope was hard to find and wire cable was equally scarce in a country at war. She was permitted to take aboard only what she actually needed for the voyage and for every piece of new rope or cable going aboard, an old piece had to come ashore.

In April, 1943, she loaded more than 204,000 packages of food destined to supplement the vitamin deficiencies of Allied war prisoners. As the ship got under way, the late A. Aubrey Bodine, a noted photographer for the *Sunday Sun*, finished a remarkable series of photographs. He had started 70 days before as the Portuguese seamen were taking down the top gallant mast and yards. Since the ship was to pass through the Chesapeake and Delaware Canal to the Delaware River, they had to be lowered to permit passage under the canal bridges. After passing through the canal they were again raised at Ready Point on the Delaware Bay. Mr. Bodine was on board when she sailed for Portugal. He went a number of miles to sea to take photographs of the Portuguese seamen hoisting the sails on the old windjammer. Because it was wartime, Mr. Bodine had to have his photographs approved for publication by the Navy and State Departments. The unforgettable photographs of a passing era were published in the *Sunday Sun* on May 23, 1943.

The schooner *Herbert L. Rawding* was built in 1919 by Atlantic Coast Company of Stockton Spring, Maine, for Crowell and Thurlow at a cost of $190,000. She was a four-masted schooner, 201 feet long with her gross tonnage of 1,219 tons. For her first ten years, she was in coastwise and West Indies trade with an occasional trans-Atlantic trip. She was sold at auction in January, 1929, for $1,600. Then, after making two trips to the West Indies, she was laid up with the idle fleet of schooners in Boothbay, Maine.

When World War II began in Europe it changed the future of all sailing freighters. The chartering rate for hauling coal from Baltimore to Martinique jumped from $2.25 a ton to $8.00 a ton. The *Rawding* was taken out of the idle fleet; overhauled and returned to the coastwise trade.

In September, 1942, she was purchased by the Inter-Continental Steamship Company of New York. Captain A. W. Schultz, port captain of the company, entered into a contract with Rukert Terminals Corporation to load the *Rawding* with general cargo consigned to Capetown, South Africa.

She arrived in Baltimore on October 1, with Captain Milton C. Decker in command, and docked at Pier 6, Locust Point Terminal of the B & O to start loading cargo. It consisted of glassware of all types, cotton piece goods from Mt Vernon Mills, drugs from local pharmaceutical houses and knocked-down empty barrels from John Eppler Company.

Under the supervision of Captains Schultz and Decker, the loading started on October 4. For the next three weeks the stevedores, with Dave Tillery as foreman and Joseph Tillery as shiprunner, loaded cargo on the schooner. Every inch of space in the cargo holds was used. The stevedores spent hours breaking open bundles of barrell staves and pushing them in every nook and corner. When a bale of cotton piece goods would not fit into a certain corner, the bale was opened and the individual pieces were used to fill that particular space. More man-hours were used in stowing this cargo aboard the schooner than normally used in loading a 10,000-ton vessel. When the hatches of the schooner were battened down, Captain Schultz was on hand and congratulated all for the excellent job of stowing.

The *Rawding* sailed from Baltimore on October 26 for Capetown. On the way down the Chesapeake Bay, she sprung a leak and put into Norfolk for repairs. After a month's delay, she sailed out of the Capes on December 15. After two days at sea the schooner began to leak badly, so she limped back to Norfolk and docked at a local shipyard. While awaiting repairs the *Rawding* was attached by the sheriff for unpaid bills. All the cargo so carefully stowed in Baltimore was removed and sold at public auction.

When that word reached the Baltimore waterfront those involved were chargrined because the many hours of hard labor in accomplishing a difficult job of stowage had gone for naught.

During the summer of 1954 the lighthouse at Lazaretto Point went dark. For 123 years it had marked the entrance to the Baltimore harbor and served as a

Lazaretto Lighthouse

navigation aid to ships sailing up the Patapsco.

It was a 34-foot high whitewashed cylindrical brick tower with a detached keeper's house built in 1831 by John Donohoo at a cost of $2,100.

Edgar Allan Poe used the lighthouse as part of a hoax which fooled hundreds of Baltimoreans. He got word around town that on April 1 a man would fly between the Shot Tower in Fells Point and Lazaretto light. Large crowds gathered at each site to see the event, and they reportedly didn't realize Poe's April Fool's joke for several hours.

In 1852 the Lighthouse Board, interested in switching to Fresnel lenses because of greater efficiency, used the light at Lazaretto as an argument for the change. Its 11 lamps with spherical reflectors used almost 450 gallons of oil annually. The board demonstrated that the smallest Fresnel lens (named after its inventor, Augustin Fresnel, a French physicist) used with only one lamp would increase the brilliance of light and result in a 900 per cent savings so the switch was made. Because iron foundries were near by, in 1870 the Lazaretto light had to be changed from red to white because the glare from the nearby smelting furnaces had colored the sky red.

In 1885 it was proposed that the Lighthouse be placed nearer the water to remove it from newly-constructed factories and warehouses. Moving would have been too costly so it was replaced with a 70-foot mast erected next to the lighthouse with a lantern suspended from its top. This was taken down three years later, and the lighthouse was reactivated. In 1916 the lighthouse became the first in Maryland or Virginia to be electrified. The property surrounding it served as the 5th Lighthouse District depot, responsible for the maintenance of aid to navigation in the Chesapeake Bay. It also served as the home berth for the lighthouse tenders *Wisteria* and *Violet*.

In the summer of 1926, a new tower, 39 feet high, with increased candlepower, was built 100 yards nearer the water. On September 29, 1926 after 95 years of service, the light in the old tower was turned off and the tower was later torn down. Many felt it should have been preserved. In addition to its role in Poe's April Fool's hoax, scholars believe, based on interior description and measurements, that the tower was the inspiration for the poet's unfinished story, "The Lighthouse."

During August 1954, the Coast Guard ordered the new light and its noisy companion, a 1,000-pound bell, decommissioned. According to the Commanding Officer of the Buoy Depot, this was done because the beacon "now sits in an industrial eclipse."

In the latter part of 1948 we were fumigating bales of imported Broom Corn 24 hours a day with methyl bromide gas. Each night I would call the superintendent to check on the operation. One night he told me that he had sent one of our top men home because he was drunk. This worried me because this man had never given us any problems in the past. Then I remembered reading, when working with this gas, that if an individual acted like he was intoxicated, it was the first sign of methyl bromide poisoning. I rushed to his house and found him lying in bed unconscious. We sent him to Johns Hopkins Hospital and told the accident room what had happened. He was quickly treated and I am happy to report he is still working for Rukert Terminals.

It was during the late 1940's and early 1950's that I noticed a slow deterioration of the port in general. Labor was demanding and receiving substantial increases in both wages and fringe benefits and the railroads which dominated the port were reluctant to upgrade their waterfront facilities.

For years the port had the reputation of being one of the finest bulk and steel ports in the United States, but times were changing. Containerization—a new type of handling general cargo—began to change the concept of cargo handling.

During the early 1950's it became apparent that some coordinating, controlling authority would have to be set up to tie together the growing number of agencies and groups engaged in port operations. A Port of Baltimore Commission was organized to provide more liberalized loans for port improvements and in 1956 the General Assembly enacted legislation establishing the Maryland Port Authority.

Shortly after the Maryland Port Authority was in operation it found itself in an embarrassing situation. My father feared that eventually it would put Rukert Terminals out of business. Six months later one of Rukert's customers informed him that the Authority had quoted a lower rate than he was charging on their commodities.

Furious, he informed everyone that he would handle the matter personally. His rough and tumble waterfront experience gave him some strong convictions and a colorful vocabulary. He was 110 percent for free enterprise and he had a healthy suspicion of government at all levels. Bureaucrats of any kind were not for him. He knew the commissioners were holding their weekly executive session in a private room in the Merchants Club, so he decided to confront them.

The confrontation is better described by Joseph L. Stanton, then the Maryland Port Administrator, which he calls "The Day the 'Cap' Painted Redwood Street Red:"

"The Maryland Port Authority luncheon meeting was proceeding in quiet fashion when the door opened with a bang and there stood 'Cap' his white plume of hair bristling, his face beet red and his eyes flashing fire. I wanted to crawl under the table. Without preamble, 'Cap' told us just what he thought of a gang of bureaucrats who would use public money (some of it his tax money, he reminded us) to undercut his fair rates and steal business away from him that he had nurtured for years. I won't try to quote 'Cap.' His vocabulary was too rich for me. He took only a couple of minutes to deliver his dressing down, but it seemed longer. His conclusion was equally colorful. Pointing to the commissioners, he yelled, 'You're all nothing but a bunch of bureaucrats and I defy you to ever try to steal any business from Rukert Terminals again.'

"That was his curtain speech. Bang went the door and he was gone, leaving a smell of fire and brimstone in the silent room. The Captain had had his say. I nearly lost my job. The commissioners were a very deflated board.

"Cap was colorful. He could be loud and belligerent, but those are only facets of a strong and remarkable man. Over the many years of our relationship, he demonstrated friendship and understanding. In his later years, he even forgave the Maryland Port Authority and its commissioners, and agreed that the authority was the right agency at the right time to restore Baltimore to its rightful place among the great seaports of the world. He loved the port only second to his family. Baltimore lost a distinguished marine leader with his passing. We are not likely to see his peer soon again."

Norman, Jr., joined the company on June 1, 1960 which made three generations working for Rukert at the same time. To keep him away from his grandfather, I arranged for the young man to join the I.L.A. checkers union so he could become a timekeeper for the company and also gain experience in the stevedoring operations.

My father, Captain W. G. N. Rukert, died on February 4, 1974 at the age of 87, after serving 66 years on the Baltimore waterfront. He was a man of unflagging energy who had devoted his life to stressing the importance of service to his customers. Port experts generally agree that he contributed more to the growth and development of maritime Baltimore than any other single person in its history.

As my son and my nephew, George Nixon, Jr., were gradually taking over the daily operations of the company it gave me an opportunity to write three successful books dealing with waterfront neighborhoods—"The Fells Point Story", in 1976; "Historic Canton", in 1978; and "Federal Hill", in 1980.

Doing the research of the Fells Point Story I was amazed to learn that Rukert Terminals owned the oldest warehouse in Baltimore and one of the oldest remaining in any U.S. port in the form of our buildings at Brown's Wharf terminal. It had been built in 1822 by James and Joseph Biays. Only the finest materials were used in the construction. The four-story building has a loft with an extreme roof pitch to eliminate snow accumulation. The bricks were imported from England and the slate for the roof came from Wales. The 18 by 12-inch beams throughout are of Georgia pine and are held in place by wooden pegs. The building had been empty for years because of the lack of elevators and increasing labor cost, so I decided to turn the historic building into a maritime museum.

It was dedicated by Mayor William Donald Schaefer of Baltimore on March 20, 1976. It proved to be a successful venture. The first day it was open to the public it had 882 visitors. The museum features a 10 by 12 foot map model of Fells Point as it appeared in the eighteenth century. Displays also include ship models, old records, coffee mugs, old photographs and paintings of vessels that were built in Baltimore. Life-size displays of nineteenth century work tools, equipment and methods are also exhibited. I have received two awards for establishing the museum: the Mayor's Award in September of 1976 and an annual preservation award of Baltimore Heritage, Inc., in December, 1979.

In January, 1980 I became Chairman of the Board and Chief Executive Officer and on June 1, 1981 finished 50 years on the Baltimore waterfront. I have continued working for the betterment of the port by serving on the Port Committee and the Port Legislative Committee of the Greater Baltimore Committee Chamber of Commerce.

World Trade Building, symbol of a new era

Sydney S. Sussman

BIBLIOGRAPHY AND CREDITS

The Port of Baltimore in the Making
by T. Courtenay J. Whedbee

History of Baltimore City & Country
by J. Thomas Scharf (Louis H. Everts 1881)

Annals of Baltimore
by Thomas W. Griffith (William Wooddy 1883)

Baltimore on the Chesapeake
by Hamilton Owens (Doubleday, Doran & Co.)

The Chronicles of Baltimore
by J. Thomas Scharf (Turnbull Bros.)

Baltimore Afire
by Harold A. Williams

Chesapeake Circle
by Robert H. Burgess (Cornell Maritime Press)

The O'Donnells of Baltimore
Published for Columbus O'Donnell Iselin, Esq. of A. Iselin & Co.

Old Baltimore
by Annie Leakin Sioussat (The Macmillan Co.)

Steamboats Out of Baltimore
by H. Graham Wood and Robert H. Burgess (Tidewater Publishers)

The Old Bay Line
by Alexander Crosby Brown (Baltimore Steam Packet Co.)

The Story of the Baltimore & Ohio Railroad
by Edward Hungerford

The Centennial History of the Pennsylvania
Railroad Company 1846–1946
by Burgess and Kennedy

Men Along The Shore
The I.L.A. and its History
by Maud Russell (Brussel & Brussel, Inc)

The Western Maryland Railway Story
A Chronicle of the First Century—1852–1952
by Harold A. Williams

CREDITS

Produced by Stanley L. Cahn
Designed by Mossman Art Studio
Typography by Monotype Composition Co.
Printed by Universal Lithographers Inc.
on Warren's Patina

INDEX

The italicized numbers refer to illustrations.

A

Abraham Rydberg (clipper) 146, 147–48
Adelaide (ship) 31, 51
Aerolite (ship) 55
Alabama (ship) 93
Albermarle (ship) 33
Alexander, Mark 16
Alum Chine (steamer) 103–4, *104*
American Radiator and Standard Sanitary Corporation 69
Amethyst (schooner) 85
Ann McKim (clipper) 27–28, *27*
Anne Arundel Docks, St. Marys City, Md. *44*
Appoquinimink Creek 81
Architect (clipper) 27, 28–29, *28*
Argonaut (submarine) 92–93
Atlantic (tugboat) 103
Atlantic and Gulf Stevedoring Company 110–11
Atlantic Steam Company 39
Atlantic Terminals 108
Atlantic Transport Company 145
Atlantis II (ship) 98–99

B

Baker, Bernard N. 129
Baker-Whitely Pier 60, 66
"Baltimore" *12–13*
Baltimore (schooner) 85
Baltimore (steamer) 57
Baltimore (tugboat) 54, 102
Baltimore and Cuba Smelting and Mining Company 34–35

Baltimore and Ohio Railroad 24–26, *25*, 55, 58–59, 60, 71–72, 79, 106–7, 110, 111, 130, 131
Baltimore and Susquehanna Railroad 26
Baltimore, Chesapeake and Richmond Steamship Company 55
Baltimore Clipper 17, *17*, 21
Baltimore Copper Smelting and Rolling Company *34*, 35
Baltimore Copper Smelting Company 35
"Baltimore from Federal Hill" *64*
Baltimore Mail Steamship Company 69–70
Baltimore Ship Repair Company 95
Baltimore Shipbuilding and Drydock Company 93
Baltimore Steam Packet Company 41, 45
Bell, Edward and Richard 30
Belt's Wharf 31
Bethlehem-Fairfield Shipyards 70–71
Bethlehem Steel Company 66
Bethlehem Steel Shipyards 91–98, *91, 92, 93, 95, 96–97*
Biays, James 151
Biays, Joseph 31, 151
Bohemia River 81
Booz and Brother, Thomas Shipyard *94*, 95
Booz, Allen and Hamilton, Inc. 136
Boston Steamship Company 40
Brewerton, Henry 73–76, *74*

Brewerton Channel 75, 76
Britannia (tugboat) 102–3
Broad Creek 81
Brown, Alexander 21
Brown, George 24, 31, 55
Brown and Collyer 41
Brown's Wharf 31, 151
Buckler, Thomas H. 23
Butler, Benjamin F. 50

C

Cambria (steamer) 51
canals 23–24
Canton (ferry) 60
Canton Company 24, 59, 63, *67*, 69, 70, 71, 114, 116
Canton Seagirt Marine Terminal *133*, 135, *135*
Carolina (ship) 31
Carrier Dover (clipper) 30
Carroll (steamer) 55
Cassard, Howard 100–2
Chase, John 142–43
Chasseur (clipper) 21
Cheeseborough, Captain 29–30
Cherokee (cutter) 46
Cherubin (clipper) 30
Chesapeake City, Md. 81
Chesapeake (steamer) 23, 39
Chesapeake and Delaware Canal 77, 81–84, *82, 83, 84*
Chesapeake Bay Steamship Line 45
Chesapeake Steamship Company 44–45
China trade 25, 28–29
Christiana Creek 81
Cigar ship 99–100, *100*
City of Baltimore (steamer) 44, 70

About the Author

Norman G. Rukert was born in Baltimore in 1915. After graduating from City College at the age of 15, he entered his father's waterfront terminal business. Over the past 5 decades his career has ranged from pier laborer to chairman of the board of Rukert Terminals Corporation, a position he attained in February 1980 after serving as president for 19 years.

He has long had an interest in historical data and restoration and today serves as vice-chairman of the Maritime Committee of the Maryland Historical Society. Under his direction, the Rukert-owned Brown's wharf, Baltimore's oldest warehouse, was renovated and established as a maritime museum in Fells Point. For this achievement, he received the Mayor's Award in 1977 and the Baltimore Heritage Award in 1979. He has recently restored a building that is an authentic late 18th century merchant's home, with the first floor serving as an exhibit hall and reception center for the maritime museum on Thames Street.

Mr. Rukert has published three books, *The Fells Point Story, Historic Canton* and *Federal Hill*, each of which treats a Baltimore neighborhood from its earliest times to the present. This is his fourth book.

Mr. Rukert was named Port Man of the Year by the Junior Chamber of Commerce in 1976 and has also received a Congressional Certificate of Merit. In 1977 he was honored with the Bell Award for Outstanding Contribution to the maritime industry. In 1979, he received the first William Fell Public Service Award for leadership in port related industry and exemplary public service. He received an honorary degree of Doctor of Humane Letters from the University of Baltimore in 1980.